LUMINOUS LIFE

How the Science of Light
Unlocks the Art of Living

JACOB ISRAEL LIBERMAN, OD, PhD

with Gina Liberman *and* Erik Liberman

Foreword by James L. Oschman, PhD

New World Library
Novato, California

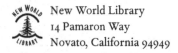 New World Library
14 Pamaron Way
Novato, California 94949

The material in this book is intended for education. It is not meant to take the place of
diagnosis and treatment by a qualified medical practitioner or therapist. No expressed
or implied guarantee of the effects of the use of the recommendations can be given or
liability taken.

Text design by Tona Pearce Myers
Illustrations by Lauren Harris, Tea Water Designs (www.teawaterdesigns.com)

Library of Congress Cataloging-in-Publication Data
Names: Liberman, Jacob, [date]- author.
Title: Luminous life : how the science of light unlocks the art of living / Jacob Israel
    Liberman, OD, PhD with Gina Liberman and Erik Liberman.
Description: Novato, California : New World Library, [2018] | Includes bibliographical
    references and index.
Identifiers: LCCN 2017044309 (print) | LCCN 2017049844 (ebook) | ISBN
    9781608685189 (Ebook) | ISBN 9781608685172 (alk. paper)
Subjects: LCSH: Light—Physiological effect—Popular works. | Vision—Physiologi-
    cal aspects—Popular works.
Classification: LCC QP82.2.L5 (ebook) | LCC QP82.2.L5 L53 2018 (print) | DDC
    612/.01444—dc23
LC record available at https://lccn.loc.gov/2017044309

First printing, February 2018
ISBN 978-1-60868-517-2
Ebook ISBN 978-1-60868-518-9

Printed in Canada on 100% postconsumer-waste recycled paper

10   9   8   7   6   5   4   3   2

Praise for Dr. Jacob Israel Liberman's Work

"Behind the disguise of brevity and simplicity lie pearls of distilled spiritual truths — truths to be cherished, to be shared, and, above all, to be lived."

> — Eckhart Tolle, author of *The Power of Now*

"Jacob Liberman is one of my favorite teachers!"

> — Louise Hay, author of *You Can Heal Your Life*

"The ideas that Jacob shares...reflect the emerging understanding... that awareness changes all experience without exception."

> — Gary Zukav, author of *The Seat of the Soul*

"I love this book [*Wisdom from an Empty Mind*]!"

> — Neale Donald Walsch, author of *Conversations with God*

"Profound and deceptively simple insights."

> — Bonnie Raitt

"It was as if I was hearing my own voice."

> — Ram Dass, author of *Be Here Now*

"Jacob Liberman...guides us into a powerfully new view of ourselves, our relationships and our inner and outer vision."

> — John Gray, PhD, author of *Men Are from Mars,*
> *Women Are from Venus*

"The sensitivity, deep humanity, and exquisite insight contained in Dr. Liberman's wonderful work make it a manual for a whole new order of being."

> — Jean Houston, author of *The Possible Human*

"Dr. Jacob Liberman is at the cutting edge of enlightened technology, blending physics and metaphysics to their best advantage. He is one of the rare breed of people in eclectic fields who have tapped in to deep wisdom principles and applied their insights and research to provide revolutionary 'new' understanding for all who 'have the eyes to see.'"

— Dan Millman, author of *Way of the Peaceful Warrior*

"Jacob Liberman's pioneer thinking takes the wonder of light and light therapy to a new level of insight by blending it with deeper health wisdom and spiritual understanding."

— Gabriel Cousens, MD, author of *Spiritual Nutrition*

"Dr. Liberman's book [*Light: Medicine of the Future*] is a milestone forward concerning the therapeutic effect of light via the eyes."

— Fritz Hollwich, MD, author of *The Influence of Ocular Light Perception on Metabolism in Man and in Animal*

"Light is one of the critical environmental factors for total health; indeed, 'the eyes are the windows of the soul.' [*Light: Medicine of the Future*] helps provide one of those windows."

— Norman Shealy, MD, founding president of the American Holistic Medical Association

"Combining his many years of personal and clinical experience with the frequently amazing results achieved by his patients, Dr. Jacob Liberman has developed a foundational model for a new medical paradigm."

— Dr. John Ott, pioneer in the field of photobiology and author of *Health and Light*

"In *Luminous Life*, Dr. Jacob Liberman articulates truths that enhance your natural brilliance and allow the intelligence of the universe to expand your lens on life."

— Donald M. Epstein, author of *The 12 Stages of Healing* and founder of EpiEnergetics

LUMINOUS
LIFE

Also by Dr. Jacob Israel Liberman

Light: Medicine of the Future

Take Off Your Glasses and See

My brain is only a receiver. In the Universe there is a core from which we obtain knowledge, strength, and inspiration. I have not penetrated into the secrets of this core, but I know that it exists.

— Nikola Tesla

CONTENTS

FOREWORD

*I*t is amazing how a simple idea can change your life. Think back on the turning points in your own personal evolution and the wonderful teachers and concepts that facilitated your awakenings to an easier, healthier, happier, and more successful life.

Many years ago, I was living with a scientist who introduced me to a very simple way of life that has made all the difference. I noticed that she did not organize her life. Instead of thinking and planning and stressing about what to do, when she got up in the morning she simply took care of the first thing that presented itself, and then the second, and so on, throughout the day. In this way she navigated effortlessly through life's adventures regardless of how challenging or complex they might be. There was no thinking, choosing, planning, or worrying about what might happen. While this sounds quite simple, in this book Dr. Jacob Israel Liberman explores this way of being in a much larger context.

In *Luminous Life*, Liberman elaborates on this relaxed and productive way of life by considering the role light plays in it: *anything that catches your eye is actually looking for you.* Light brings your awareness to your responsibilities, guides you from moment to moment, and creates a life filled with purpose and meaning. "We need not prioritize anything, because the intelligence of life has already done that for us." Living in this space is what he refers to as *presence*. "Not knowing...allows true wisdom to reveal itself." The landmark book you have in your hands documents these concepts and much more.

Liberman explains how this approach to daily life enables us to allow light — and its faithful companion, breath — to guide us and to "see the inner workings of our lives with greater clarity and acceptance." He cites ancient wisdom summarized by Mahatma Gandhi: "There is a force in the universe, which, if we permit it, will flow through us and produce miraculous results" (chapter 4).

My current research involves documenting the science behind this "force in the universe." Liberman's writings have greatly facilitated my process of discovery. He points out that this force animates "the navigational system within us" that is "inseparable from that which animates everything in the universe." Surrendering to "pure awareness" of this force can lead to miracles and profound healing. "Many of our physical and emotional ailments are the result of our bodies being misdirected by ideas that are in conflict with our well-being" (chapter 8).

Luminous Life will give you a totally new perspective on the many roles of light and breath in your personal evolution — on what it truly means to *see*. It will help you uncover your purpose or destiny and how living it brings forth your essence, changing your world and the world around you. I like to say that when you are "on purpose" or following your destiny, the wind will fill your sails and the tools you need will appear.

Much of Liberman's storytelling begins with an account of an experience that led to a simple and penetrating but rarely asked question, followed by an answer that can be as startling as it is revealing.

For example, he asks about the source of the light we experience in our dreams. Dreams reveal how the rainbows of our inner light interact with our subconscious mind to expose deep truths about our waking experiences, as well as our "limitless nature" (chapter 5). Tapping into these clues about how our stories and beliefs shape our waking actions leads us to greater clarity and more enlightened behavior.

Liberman cites the *Talmud*: "We do not see things as they are; we see them as we are." Suspending our beliefs about who we are and what is possible creates a luminous space that allows us to open to *pure awareness*; to infinite potentials and possibilities; to discovering the true genius within us. Unconscious inspirations, in cooperation with conscious activities, can lead to excitation, followed by implementation, leading to creative manifestation (chapter 7). This is the true source of inspired action. As Einstein stated, to be creative "imagination is more important than knowledge."

Liberman discusses "the zone" — a state of consciousness experienced by elite athletes, musicians, dancers, and so on when they are having a flawless performance (chapter 8). In 1992 I had an experience that brought my career into congruence with Liberman's work with top athletes to get them into "the zone" more readily. I was watching the Olympic skating championships when figure skater Midori Ito took my breath away and brought me to tears with a moving and legendary performance. Despite some difficult practice sessions preceding the competition, she began her routine radiating complete calmness and control. Her program included a triple-triple jump combination and a triple axel, the first time a female figure skater accomplished these feats in an Olympic competition. This thrilling experience was the beginning of my inquiry that led to the publication of my 2003 book, *Energy Medicine in Therapeutics and Human Performance*, and to the recognition of a state of consciousness and physiology that I call "systemic cooperation." In "the zone" all tissues and cells and molecules throughout the body work together naturally, quickly, effortlessly, and instinctually, enabling the performer to embody complete aliveness, presence, clarity, and grace. In this book, Liberman provides one-minute meditations that help all of us enter "the zone" and live there. *What a gift!*

For all parts of the body to cooperate so perfectly some form of rapid cell-to-cell communication must be taking place. Light provides the perfect communication mechanism for high-speed physiological integration because it travels at the speed of light. Recently the new multidisciplinary study of biophotonics has emerged. Liberman's research and insights into light and vision are vital to biophoton research.

Dr. Jacob Israel Liberman is a true pioneer and visionary. His work with vision has led to valuable insights about light and sight, uncovering new ways of seeing and living. I cannot imagine a more sacred and gratifying journey than helping people maintain what is their most precious gift: their sight. Some of Liberman's discoveries were so remarkable that he was compelled to do careful scientific research to convince himself of their validity. The result has been a series of outstanding articles published in peer-reviewed scientific journals, establishing him as one of the world's most creative and highly regarded vision scientists. In *Luminous Life: How the Science of Light Unlocks the Art of Living*, Liberman makes his extraordinary discoveries available to all of us. This is far more than a book to read and enjoy — it is a life-changing journey.

— James L. Oschman, PhD, author of
Energy Medicine: The Scientific Basis

INTRODUCTION

*F*orty years ago, while practicing as an optometrist, I experienced a sudden and very significant improvement in eyesight, with no measurable change in my eyeglass prescription. The effect of that miraculous event, which has now persisted for forty years, led me to the realization that while we look with our eyes, we do not "see" with them. This spurred me on a mission to discover the source of our true seeing: the connection between light, vision, and consciousness. Most importantly, it led me to ask, who am I, and who is truly the seer?

These questions drew me to study quantum physics and neuroscience, which inspired me to deeply explore the state of mind that led to my profound vision improvement. So I began a real-time experiment on the workings of my mind. My hope was to uncover a *portal* into the state of consciousness where profound healing occurs, which in turn would allow me to teach others how to replicate my experience. What I discovered over the years transformed my life and revealed some fundamental truths about light and vision. These insights allowed me to assist thousands of patients in restoring their natural eyesight without the use of glasses, forming the basis of my first two books, *Light: Medicine of the Future* and *Take Off Your Glasses and See*.

What followed over the next twenty-five years was a profound exploration into life, consciousness, and that elusive state we call *presence*. My discoveries, presented herein, helped me unravel how light continually guides our life. In addition, those breakthroughs were foundational to my development in 2006 of the first patented, clinically proven, and FDA-cleared medical device that significantly improved vision performance and contributed to my induction as president of the International Society for the Study of Subtle Energies and Energy Medicine (ISSSEEM) in 2010.

Light's Guidance

To better understand my findings, let's start with light and a broader understanding of it. Light is more than waves and particles. It is a purveyor of consciousness. Light is not just "out there," something we need to find in order to see. *Light seeks us out* and guides us in the same way it seeks out and directs a plant to grow toward it. There is something inherently alive in it. And, astonishing as it might seem, light not only enters us through our eyes and skin but also *emanates from within us*. Consider how babies perceive the world around them. Light ignites their awareness — unobstructed by thought, belief, or worry — and it radiates back into the world as an expression of pure *presence*. That is why their eyes sparkle. As we grow from babies who exist in this unfettered state into adults who are taught to look for life, love, and work, we overlook the fact that our eyes and minds are not designed to look for light but to respond to it.

Pioneering experiments have confirmed that the eyes, which contain approximately one billion working parts, not only detect single photons of light before they take shape in form but also assimilate and distribute that information to our brains at unimaginable speeds.

This entire process occurs before the conscious mind thinks about it and directs us toward what to look at. In addition, researchers have found cryptochrome, the chemical "sixth sense" that orients animals with the earth's electromagnetic field, at highly concentrated levels in the human eye, calibrating us with the unseen "clock and compass" that guides group migrations of many species and even their reproductive cycles.

Looking for Presence

Despite popular belief, attaining presence is not about thinking or trying to *be here now*. Rather, it is a naturally occurring state that arises when our eyes and mind, triggered by light, focus on the same place at the same time. In response to light's invitation and guidance, our eyes begin an intricate dance of *aiming*, *focusing*, *tracking*, and *teaming*. When light first "awakens" us, our eyes *aim* toward its emanation, initiating an all-encompassing *presence*. Though we often relate presence to attention, it has no tension associated with it. It is not a forced voluntary process of selecting one aspect of our environment to focus on while ignoring others. Presence is an involuntary response to an invitation by life's intelligence pointing us toward our maximum potential.

Our degree of presence is directly related to how effortlessly and accurately our eyes are able to aim. When the eyes aim effectively, making eye contact with — and thus, acknowledging — what has called to them, we experience *congruence*. This is a state of coming together, the perfect alignment of our outer and inner worlds, where extraneous noise around us diminishes.

I discovered this during my career as an optometrist and vision scientist. When patients came to me with vision problems, I found that most of the time their eyes would look at one spot, but their mind would be elsewhere. This incongruity between what their eyes and their mind were seeing interfered with their natural ability to experience presence. In one of my research studies, published in 1976, I found that nearly 70 percent of the participants were not looking where they thought they were looking, a sign that their eyes and mind were not converged on the same point. In addition, more than half of the subjects were looking too hard, revealing a tendency to push rather than allow things to unfold before their eyes. I also observed that the more my patients worked at seeing or understanding something, the more they held their breath and the less they actually saw. However, when their natural breathing cycle was restored, they relaxed and their vision and learning ability significantly improved.

This is why presence is so rare. When our physical eyes (which receive 80 to 90 percent of our life experience) are not aligned with our "mind's eye," it is impossible to experience presence or oneness. If you are middle-aged or older and have taken to using reading glasses, then you likely know what it feels like to try to read the small print on the label of a supplement container at the pharmacy without your reading glasses. The harder you try, the more your eyes strain. Yet the text on the container still does not come into focus. The way to see the text more clearly lies in releasing your effort and softening your focus, allowing your mind and your eyes to naturally align themselves. You cannot force this, but you can learn how to allow it naturally with a simple one-minute vision exercise that I reveal later in this book.

Using just a string and a few beads, you can *see* my point and directly experience your eyes and mind aligning, not by forcing the process but by allowing it. Since *awareness is curative*, once you have experienced it, you will not go back to your old way of seeing or being.

Are You Allergic to Life?

Another reason why presence often eludes us is due to our emotional pain, or what I refer to as our allergies to life. Presence is difficult to experience if you have learned to brace against it or attempt to escape what life presents or triggers in you. Presence is not about picking and choosing your experience: yes, I will be present to this; no, I will not be present to that. The intelligence of life is constantly directing us toward *presence*. It is our opportunity to experience how life guides us in each and every moment, allowing us to breathe easily. Yet early-life traumas along with our emotional predispositions cause us to automatically recoil from particular people and situations. We are usually not aware of why this is happening. All we see are people and experiences that feel scary, uncomfortable, or overwhelming to us.

This is where the science of light and life magically unite, because we tend to respond to color in the same way we respond to life. Throughout my career I found that my patients were allergic to the colors that, on a vibrational level, corresponded to the life experiences they found difficult to process. So when they viewed those colors, they had reactions that affected them physically and emotionally, filling their minds and blocking their connection to *presence*. Once they used "color homeopathy," which I will explain and demonstrate later in the book, and were able to embrace the colors that previously had caused reactions, they were able to experience greater presence with the life experiences that previously triggered them.

What Is Catching Your Eye?

I learned a great deal from observing my children when they were very young. Like most children, they often played with toys, leaving them out when they were finished. I repeatedly asked them to put their toys away, which only seemed to work when I insisted. I then had a strong feeling that *if I see it, it is my responsibility*. I began wondering what would happen if I started responding to everything that *caught my eye*. So I began an around-the-clock practice that went like this: anything that entered my awareness became my responsibility, anything that was my responsibility I would attend to, and anything I attended to I would complete. I did this practice for a week and did not let anything get by me; by Sunday, I was picking up cigarette butts off the street.

After that week I was a more contented person. I realized how much time I had spent worrying about my circumstances, hoping they would change. But whenever I tried to decide what to do next, there was never any clarity. During this experiment, however, clarity emerged *on its own*, as whatever called to me became the next logical thing to do. This practice in *presence* — a kind of *moving meditation* — made me feel that I no longer needed to prioritize my schedule because *life had already done that*, drawing my awareness to whatever required its attention. In addition, my presence — and in turn, my vision — deepened as I stopped ignoring what I was seeing. I had the sense then that ignoring what we see might actually be at the root of much of the vision loss I saw in my practice. In this book you will be encouraged to perform an exercise to "see" for yourself just how life-changing something so simple can be. In no time at all, a renewed sense of spaciousness and ease emerges.

I now know that life is continuously serving us our curriculum, and if we naturally respond moment by moment to what is calling us, we not only will experience an amazing state of grace and presence, but we will also develop a real sense of self-respect, knowing that we will meet whatever life brings head-on. By living *choicelessly* we benefit from the guiding compass of the universe, experiencing less stress and more joy, inspiration, love, and gratitude.

Merging with Life

My first two books, *Light: Medicine of the Future* and *Take Off Your Glasses and See*, shared revolutionary ideas, therapeutic treatments, and a directory of practitioners who offered these modalities.

Luminous Life: How the Science of Light Unlocks the Art of Living combines forty-five years of clinical research and direct experience with contemporary science to create a new philosophy of life that can be implemented and integrated by you at home, resulting in transformation that is rapid, significant, and permanent.

Luminous Life explores the connection between light, vision, and consciousness, and its inseparable impact on *presence*. It brings you to the intersection of science and spirituality, quantum physics and mysticism, and neuroscience and Eastern philosophy. Grounded in science, supported by research and personal experience, it reformulates two millennia of spiritual wisdom into a practical philosophy along with the tools to help you finally experience that elusive and profound state we call *presence*.

When we "work" at being present, we remain locked in a pattern of excessive effort and thinking. Rather than responding to light's invitation to full awareness, we remain lost in thought, plans, and anxiety, and we see the world through the tunnel vision created by those concerns. Those thoughts lock our reality into place, freezing light into matter.

If we stop trying to be present and instead tap into our breath, align our eyes and mind congruently, and respond to life's invitations, *presence finds us*. Presence is what arises when we embrace all that life (and light) has to offer. When we stop searching, we start finding. By looking less, we see more. When we allow the light within us to merge with the light that guides us, we experience oneness. Without any effort, we relax into a state where we have no decisions to make. There is no confusion, second-guessing, thinking, or searching for answers. There is just beingness — an acceptance of life as it is.

With presence, life becomes magical. We not only feel better, but our stress dissipates and our bodies heal. We respond to life more fluidly, developing an ability to be with whatever arises, flowing in response to life in the same way that children do. Infants and children do not look for anything; they simply respond to whatever calls their attention. When we reawaken this innate ability in ourselves, our lives transform radically. We enter a state that some call "the zone," "the flow," or even "genius consciousness," in which "we" disappear and our knowledge is no longer limited to information received from the five senses. We become more empathetic toward ourselves and others, and more intuitive. Rather than reacting to one situation after another, we start flowing with life and, over time, we become increasingly aware of experiences just before they occur and can now "welcome" them. It is a miraculous state of being.

What you might call the "divine inspiration" encoded in light moves us in a direction that is expansive, infusing us with a deep desire — beyond the wish for anything personal or material — to embrace our most potent longing for oneness with the vision we have been given. There remains only a *witness* who is present, spacious, and imperturbable. Everything appears clear and seems to scintillate. The resulting sense of peace is so blissful that it may bring tears to our eyes.

No matter how many miracles we experience, each new wonder is always astounding, inviting in more such experiences and reminding us that all of life is literally *beyond belief.* Over the past twenty-five years I have been transformed from an eye doctor and vision scientist to an "I" doctor fascinated by consciousness and the science of life. Barely a day goes by that I am not in awe of this marvelous world we live in and the people I encounter. I am excited to share what I have learned because it has transformed my life, and I believe it can transform yours as well.

CHAPTER ONE

How Light Guides Us

Whether in the intellectual pursuits of science or in the mystical pursuits of the spirit, the light beckons ahead, and the purpose surging in our nature responds.

— ARTHUR STANLEY EDDINGTON

At daybreak in a large lake on the island of Palau in the Philippine Sea, a dance begins. Millions of golden jellyfish, each the size of a teacup, race east toward the light of the rising sun. Once they reach the sun's early morning rays, they halt. Then slowly, as the sun makes its way east to west, the jellies follow its arc. As dusk falls these unique invertebrates come to rest on the lake's western shore. The following morning, the dance begins again.

These jellies are just one of countless species whose life journeys are guided by the sun's light. According to marine biologists, humpback whales use sunlight, along with the stars and the earth's magnetic pull, to guide their ten-thousand-mile yearly migrations. Despite ocean currents, the whales swim in a straight line — north to feed and south to mate — varying less than one degree longitude from year to year.

Each fall in Antarctica, emperor penguins march, single file, on a treacherous seventy-mile journey inland to their breeding grounds. Once there, they pair off and mate. After the female lays an egg, she carefully transfers it to the feet of the male, who incubates it in the space between the base of his belly and the top of his feet. The female then returns to the ocean in search of food. For two months, the males huddle together without food, balancing the eggs on top of their feet, while temperatures descend to one hundred degrees below zero Fahrenheit and wind speeds reach one hundred miles per hour. In an intricate dance, the males on the inside of the group move toward the periphery as their body temperatures rise, while those on the outside gradually move in to get warm. Later, after the females return and the chicks hatch, the penguins trek en masse seventy miles back to the sea, as if they were one organism — each one a cell in an intricately connected body of life.

In addition to jellies, whales, and penguins, many other creatures — ranging from butterflies to songbirds — take part in extraordinary migratory journeys guided by something outside themselves that is inseparably aligned with something inside them. When we learn about such feats, we often marvel at these creatures' amazing ability to travel from point A to point B. In the absence of maps, printed directions, and GPS technology, how do they find their way to their locations — never varying their routes, never getting lost, never second-guessing themselves, and never bickering with one another about the right route to take?

Most of us only hear about these stories on the Discovery channel or from documentaries such as *March of the Penguins.* But when we come upon this phenomenon in our own lives, it stops us in our tracks and makes us realize that we miss a lot of activity happening around us.

When I moved into a rented cottage on Maui, Hawaii, some years ago, I found a little Russian Blue cat with gray fur and yellow eyes sitting on the porch staring at me. I learned that she was feral and that my neighbor Koa called her Pepper, and that she came by around the same time every day. I bought a few cans of cat food from a nearby market, opened one, and left it on the porch. She gobbled it up, so I left food and water on the porch and each day Pepper came to eat. This went on for five months, and we began to grow friendly toward one another.

One day I saw Koa carrying a cardboard box with Pepper inside. "Where are you taking her?" I asked.

"I have a friend on the other side of the island who wants her."

The friend lived thirty-five miles away, and though I was fond of Pepper, I knew it was for the best as I was leaving for Europe within a few days.

Three months later, after a friend picked me up from the airport and drove me back to the cottage, I found Pepper waiting there for me.

Surprised, I stepped over to Koa's cottage. "When did you bring Pepper back?"

"I didn't."

Together we walked back to my cottage. Once he saw the cat, Koa said, "Oh my God." Then he called his friend and asked, "Why did you bring the cat back?"

The friend replied, "I didn't. She ran away almost as soon as you dropped her off. I never saw her again."

Amazed that she had found her way home at the very moment I arrived, I renamed her Lani, which means "heaven" in Hawaiian. Soon I moved to a new home and I took her with me.

To us, such a journey sounds impossible, especially if we often find ourselves lost within an unfamiliar city or even just within a mall parking lot. In reality, we humans are equipped with the same guidance technology as jellies, whales, and these other amazing creatures. Birds, for instance, appear to have a built-in compass in their eyes, as their retinas contain high concentrations of the light-sensitive protein cryptochrome, which affords them the ability to detect the earth's magnetic field. But cryptochrome is not unique to birds; it is a prehistoric protein found in microbes, plants, and animals that helps control daily rhythms and the detection of magnetic fields in an increasing number of species. Some researchers believe that birds can actually *see* these invisible fields superimposed above their normal vision.

Humans were thought to have only five senses, while animals such as birds, whales, and turtles had a sixth sense that allows them to orient themselves during these long migrations. Recently, however, a team of scientists from the University of Massachusetts Medical School found that the human eye also contains high concentrations of cryptochrome. Moreover, when the human cryptochrome gene is implanted into a fruit fly, after its normal magnetic sixth sense has been altered, it restores its ability to sense magnetic fields like its normal peers. These experiments demonstrate that human cryptochrome can act as a magnetic sensor, suggesting that we too may be equipped with such a sixth sense, aligning us with the intricate navigational system of the planet.

One obvious difference between these animals and us: they do not override their inner guidance system with thinking. They do not question the arc of the sun. They do not choose to follow or not follow it. They not trust the light, nor do they distrust it. They merely follow the light as it leads them to their destination. But this begs the question: What is light?

What Is Light?

Since humanity's first sunrise, seers have wondered about the nature of light and suspected that this mysterious and all-pervasive phenomenon must be fundamentally related to our deepest questions about God, life, and the meaning of existence. The Bible tells us that life began with the dawning of light, and virtually every spiritual tradition identifies light with the Creator, speaking of the "divine light," the "light of God," and describing spiritual evolution as the process of "enlightenment."

Health and well-being are commonly thought of as an emanation of light — or "glow" — a radiance that cannot be described.

Glowing physical health is primarily a function of the power of our "inner sun," and our glow seems to increase as our awareness expands. At full illumination, this radiance becomes visible to the naked eye, which is why great actors are often likened to "stars," and saints are traditionally depicted as being surrounded by brilliant halos and described as "illumined."

Many of our verbal expressions also illustrate the countless ways in which light manifests in our everyday lives. We say that pregnant women are "glowing," and when we feel inspired we say we have had a "flash" of insight. When someone is very smart, we say they are "brilliant"; and when they have changed their beliefs or thinking, we say they have "seen the light." When we speak of a new idea, we might say "a light bulb went off." When we want someone to calm down, we might suggest they "lighten up."

Scientists have also puzzled over the nature of light. In 1640 the Italian astronomer Galileo wrote a letter to philosopher Fortunio Liceti stating, "I have always considered myself unable to understand what light was, so much so that I would readily have agreed to spend the rest of my life in prison with only bread and water if only I could have been sure of reaching the understanding that seems so hopeless to me." Around 1917 the physicist Albert Einstein wrote to a friend, "For the rest of my life I will reflect on what light is!" By 1951 he confessed that he had spent fifty years of "conscious brooding," trying to understand the nature of light yet was no closer to the answer than when he began.

In the process of chasing the mystery of light, however, Einstein developed the theory of relativity, establishing that at the speed of light, time ceases to exist. In addition, a photon, which has no mass, can cross the cosmos without using any energy. So for light beams, time and space do not exist.

More recently, however, quantum physicists have described light as the foundation of reality. This is profoundly significant when we realize that quantum theory is considered the most successful scientific formulation in history and that 50 percent of our current technology is based on it. According to theoretical physicist David Bohm, "Light is energy and it's also information, content, form, and structure. It's the potential of everything."

We live in a universe that appears to be created and nourished by light. According to German writer and politician Johann Wolfgang von Goethe, "All life originates and develops under the influence of...light." This becomes obvious when we experimentally place plants, animals, or humans in darkened environments and notice that their vitality and well-being gradually diminish, bringing their lives to a halt. Without light, there is no will to live. We are literally robbed of the spark that propels our spirit.

With such recognitions, the artificial distinctions we have between science, health care, and spirituality are dissolving, and each is being traced back to *light*. Mystics, scientists, and healers now agree, in their respective terms, that light holds the secret to human awakening, healing, and transformation. Yet we still do not understand what light is.

Light is made up of photons, and it is believed that subatomic particles are composed of photons, which are the fundamental building blocks of what we call matter or reality. Photons are formless, invisible, and without attributes. They have no mass, weight, or electrical charge, and thus cannot be directly perceived or measured.

That is why we never truly *see light*. And yet everything we see, hear, smell, and touch is made of photons. According to American polymath and author Walter Russell, not only is seeing "a sensation of feeling light waves through our eyes," but "hearing is a sensation of feeling light waves through our ears. Tasting and smelling are sensations of feeling light waves reacting upon mouth and nostrils."

David Bohm took things a step further when he stated, "All matter is frozen light." The quantum reality Bohm describes is founded on a simple principle: light and life are the same energy in two different states of existence, form (matter) and formlessness (light). In its formed or frozen state, light energy composes all the matter in the universe — everything we see, touch, and measure. Bohm's statement refers to the transformation of light into matter — how light becomes life, its potential energy, described by Einstein's famous equation $E=mc^2$. What is just as important, however, is how life or matter can, once again, become light.

You might be able to more easily picture the seamless interplay between the form and the formless if you think of plants and how they are guided and transformed by light throughout their life cycle.

First, a plant "sees" where light is emanating and naturally positions itself to be in optimal alignment with it. This ability to sense different qualities and quantities of light is crucial to a plant's survival, as it ensures the leaves are in prime position to collect sunlight with the least effort while guiding the roots toward soil with its ideal moisture.

This miraculous process of a plant being in the right place at the right time facilitates the process of photosynthesis, whereby sunlight bonds carbon dioxide (CO_2) and water (H_2O) to create sugar, the essential fuel that powers organic systems. When humans and animals consume plants, that bond is dissolved once again, dividing sugar into carbon dioxide and water. The carbon dioxide is then eliminated via the lungs, and the water via perspiration and urination, leaving only light within the organism.

In essence, we live on sunlight. Plants absorb the formless energy of light from the sun and store it in their leaves. When we eat those plants, we literally ingest *frozen light*, use it, and what remains is its formless essence... *light*.

In the second edition of his book *Opticks*, published in 1717, Sir Isaac Newton says, "Are not gross bodies and light convertible into one another; and may not bodies receive much of their activity from the particles of light which enter into their composition? The changing of bodies into light, and light into bodies, is very conformable to the course of Nature, which seems delighted with transmutations."

We respond to light like plants, continuously moving toward greater alignment with the light and the consciousness that underlies it, while interacting with the qualities and quantities of light that best support our physical, emotional, and spiritual development. We are all creatures of light.

How Light Guides Us

In this very moment, light is guiding your eyes to these words, illuminating meaning and creating a connection between you and this book. That connection is called *presence*. Without light you would not be able to see these words. They simply would not appear to your eyes. Light literally brings the words to you, creating a sense of inseparability between perception and meaning. The light that brings you the words you read also brings "to light" the people, situations, and opportunities required to spur your evolution. It takes you by the hand and leads you where you need to be and when you need to be there. And light's guidance has no side effects. However, we must remember how to recognize it.

It is the same with everything we see. Light — from the sun, from lamps, from fire — reflects off objects and interacts with our eyes, releasing energy and information about those objects, which are then magically transformed into an image that appears full of light. But, it is not actually light. It is just a mental interpretation that we experience as brightness.

Many people think of the eyes as two cameras mounted on the face, but in reality they are elaborate and complex extensions of the brain, and each of these extensions is designed to both absorb and emit light. Each eye contains 126 million photoreceptors. Approximately 95 percent of these receptors (called rods) are distributed spaciously throughout the retina. The other 5 percent (called cones) are primarily compacted into a tiny area called the macula. Rods are extremely sensitive, functioning under low-level light conditions and responding to motion. Cones are less sensitive, adapted to color perception and high-resolution vision.

Based on their design, rods seem to be able to sense things before our conscious mind registers their form. In fact, researchers from Rockefeller University and the Research Institute of Molecular Pathology in Austria recently demonstrated that the human eye can detect a single photon of light. Since a photon is the smallest undividable unit of energy, this discovery clearly confirms that our eyes are designed to operate at the quantum level of reality, and our vision has been honed by evolution to function at its maximum potential.

Yet photons are technically invisible. They do not create an image that the brain can see, yet this minute amount of light still "calls" the eye, giving new meaning to eighteenth-century essayist Jonathan Swift's statement, "Real vision is the ability to see the invisible." In response to this infinitesimally subtle invitation, the eye reflexively moves toward that which is calling it, and it does this without our conscious awareness. According to Alipasha Vaziri, the study's lead researcher, "The most amazing thing is that it's not like seeing light. It's almost a feeling, at the threshold of imagination."

Cones inspect things carefully when the situation demands it but require significantly brighter light to do so. So when your optometrist asks you which is better, number one or number two, your cones allow you to know the difference. As you can see, vision is primarily a global process that continuously aligns us with the greater whole and zeros in on details only when necessary. Our life experiences are primarily the result of the ongoing interaction that links our eyes with light.

The process of vision — our response to what we see — begins within a few quadrillionths of a second after light enters the eye, enabling the information encoded in light to be transmitted to, and interpreted by, the brain and all systems connected to it at light speed. We might think, "Look at that car." In reality, light bounced off the car, attracted our eye, entered our brain, and sent signals down various nerve endings long before the thought "Look at that" surfaced. Hence the wisdom behind the expression "It caught my eye." Yet rarely do we ask what the "it" is to which we are referring. My sense is that this "it" is the same light the Bible refers to as "God," and quantum physicists describe as the formless bedrock of consciousness guiding every step of our lives — the intelligence of life.

Light guides more than just our eyesight. It also guides our breathing, our heartbeat, our sleep-wake cycle, and much more. The eye contains nonvisual, light-sensing cells that are developed and functioning long before the rods and cones that process light into vision are operative. In fact, these cells may be present at birth, confirming that light entering the eyes directs our body's homeodynamic process from the earliest stages of life.

When light enters the eyes, the entire brain lights up because the light does not just travel to the brain's visual cortex, enabling us to see. It travels along several different routes that involve the entire brain, significantly affecting all our life-sustaining functions as well as our emotions, balance, and coordination, to name a few. For example, light entering the eyes goes to the "brain's brain," the hypothalamus, which regulates the autonomic nervous system and the endocrine system, as well as our reaction and adaptation to stress. Using light-activated information, the hypothalamus communicates with the body's true "master gland," the pineal. The pineal is the same structure that allows humpback whales to use light during their annual migrations.

Referred to as the "third eye" by Indian mystics and the "seat of the soul" by seventeenth-century mathematician and philosopher Descartes, the pineal gland, the body's "regulator of regulators," shares information about environmental light changes and the earth's electromagnetic field with every cell of the body at the same instance of time. In doing so, each cell effortlessly upgrades and synchronizes its function with Mother Nature, bringing us to our natural state of oneness with no effort or thinking required.

So when light contacts the body's energy field, it resonates first with the pineal. The pineal, acting as the conductor of the endocrine symphony, then entrains the pituitary, thyroid, thymus, pancreas, gonads, and adrenals, translating light energy into electricity, magnetism, and eventually to chemical energy itself. It has now been confirmed that the order of endocrine entrainment in the human body correlates completely with ancient medical systems that describe the workings of the body's major energy centers or chakras.

In addition to the visual and nonvisual effects of light by way of the eyes, light also guides the trillions of cells in our body via a process called photobiomodulation, catalyzing a cascade of events that stimulate and/or inhibit cellular activity down to the DNA. This process reveals that when the cell's powerhouse, the mitochondria, absorbs light, it significantly impacts the production of adenosine triphosphate. This is the energy used by cells to power the metabolic processes that create DNA, ribonucleic acid, proteins, and enzymes, as well as other biological materials required to repair or regenerate cellular components, nurture cell division, and restore homeostasis.

All biological life is composed of, and dependent on, light. The term *solar system* means "of or derived from the sun." In fact, 98 percent of the sun's light enters the body through the eyes, and the other 2 percent enters by way of the skin. Thus, light is the primal nourishment for life. The body is a biological light receptor, the eyes are transparent biological windows designed to receive and emit light, and all physiological functions are light dependent. For example, routine exposure to sunlight reduces resting heart rate, respiratory rate, blood pressure, and blood sugar, while increasing energy, strength, endurance, stress tolerance, and the ability of the blood to absorb and carry oxygen.

After forty-five years of investigating light and its therapeutic applications, I have concluded that the intelligence of life summons us through light, guiding and illuminating our entire life's journey. Light and life are inseparable.

CHAPTER TWO

The Light within Us

Each one of you has a priceless treasure: there is light emanating from your eyes, which illuminates mountains, rivers, and the great earth.
— ZEN MASTER CHANGQING DA'AN

O ur eyes not only absorb light, but they also reflect and emit it, causing our eyes to literally light up under certain conditions and appear dim under others. Think of the last time you interacted with a baby. Perhaps after you made some cooing sounds or funny faces, you focused on the baby's eyes and noticed their sparkle. Yet when you look at someone who is in distress or is not feeling well, their eyes seem to have lost their luster. What's behind this phenomenon? As is often attributed to Shakespeare, the eyes are the windows of the soul.

In chapter 1, we saw that many creatures take part in extraordinary journeys guided by something outside them that is inseparably aligned with something inside them. Our life journey is also guided in the same way by light. When this alignment happens, a state of oneness known as *presence* arises within us; our eyes light up and the next step of our journey becomes evident.

I first became aware of this phenomenon during my third year of optometric training, when prominent behavioral optometrist John

W. Streff visited Southern College of Optometry. At the time, Streff was the director of vision research at the Gesell Institute of Child Development at Yale. He had become known for describing a constellation of visual symptoms that resulted from stress and that is now called the Streff syndrome. Shortly after he arrived, Streff was casually chatting with a group of students and a journalist in the student union when he asked, "Could I have a volunteer?" The journalist, a young man in his twenties, raised his hand.

Dr. Streff used a sophisticated piece of equipment called a retinoscope to shine light into the journalist's eye so he could observe the reflection (or "reflex") of light off the retina.

"I want you to imagine that you are playing tennis," Dr. Streff said.

As the man imagined, Dr. Streff peered through the top of the retinoscope, his face about twenty inches from the man's eyes. A few moments of quiet anticipation passed. Then Dr. Streff said, "You just hit the ball...there, you hit another one...and another one."

He was joking, I thought. After all, how could Dr. Streff know when this journalist was imagining hitting a ball?

"There, you hit it...you hit it again," Dr. Streff continued to announce.

The man began to laugh. We all began to laugh too, although we did not yet know why. Then the journalist exclaimed, "You told me what I was doing just before I did it in my mind!"

Although this may sound strange, in a recently published paper in the journal *PLOS Biology*, an international team of researchers suggests that a lag exists between seeing something and becoming aware of it. According to the new "time slice theory," supported by previously published psychological and behavioral experiments, our brains process unconscious information in brief frames of time and then splice the frames together like a movie into what we perceive as a continuous flow of conscious information.

In essence, we do not experience stimuli when they actually

occur but much later, relatively speaking, when we become conscious of them. Another way of saying this is that our eyes respond to light well before it is rendered into our conscious experience of life. As we become increasingly more aware of the "just noticeable differences" occurring within us and in the world around us, we respond to subtler and subtler aspects of life, eventually seeing what is invisible to others.

I did not realize it then, but Dr. Streff's awareness was highly developed, allowing him to notice when the light emitted from his retinoscope fused with the light emitted from the journalist's eyes, providing him insights the journalist was not yet aware of.

"Let's do it again," Dr. Streff said. The journalist continued to visualize a game of tennis.

"That was a forehand," Dr. Streff said.

"Nice backhand," he continued. "Oh, you just hit a lob," and on the commentary went.

Blown away by the demonstration, we all started talking at once, asking question after question. That day it became clear to me that there was an aspect of vision that had nothing to do with eye exams or glasses. I had had many experiences during my life where I sensed something before it occurred. But I could not imagine, at the time, how by peering into someone's eyes Dr. Streff seemed able to see what another person was imagining. I was so inspired that I offered to drive Dr. Streff everywhere he went during his visit so I could question him.

Soon after Dr. Streff's demonstration, a six-year-old girl was brought to the college clinic because she was failing in school and was a bit clumsy. Her parents assumed poor eyesight was to blame. Like Dr. Streff before me, I used a retinoscope to peer into the young girl's eyes. I watched her eyes as I put different strength lenses in front of them. The eyes of most patients usually reflexively change as different strength lenses change the appearance of the eye chart in front of them, but the eyes of this young girl were nearly static.

Her eye reflexes were dull, and her eyes appeared dark, as if no light was getting in or out. She could not see, but there was no biological reason for her poor eyesight. No matter what prescription I tried, her eyes did not respond. It was as if nothing could touch her, and I began to wonder if she might have suffered a trauma that was clouding her eyesight.

Although I was just beginning my third year of optometry school, I had read in one of my textbooks that emotional issues could, at times, produce a temporary loss of vision termed *hysterical blindness*. It became clear to me that glasses were not going to help her, so I removed my white clinic jacket, sat on the floor, and did something I had never done.

"Do you know your letters and numbers?" I asked.

She said that she did.

"Great, then let's play a game! I am going to use my finger to write a number on your back. I want you to tell me the number, okay?"

Lightly, with my index finger, I drew a number one. She seemed confused.

I turned around. "How about you do it to me? Draw a letter or a number on my back and see if I can guess what it is."

By the end of that session I could already see a change. It was as if she opened a door and allowed me into her world. She trusted me because I helped her discover that she could see via her feelings rather than just her eyes. Her eyes seemed brighter, and she was already starting to guess the right letters and numbers. For a few weeks I continued to work with her in this way. By the end of the tenth session, I could draw three-letter words and double-digit numbers on her back, and she could guess correctly most of the time. She could track a ball with her eyes, walk on a balance beam, and see with 20/20 vision. It was obvious that she was seeing the world differently and so was I.

Later during my career, I began asking patients to complete

different tasks as I watched their eyes. The patients read. They did math in their heads. They imagined. Initially, as expected, I noticed that the pupil would dilate and constrict in response to light, as if it was actually breathing. Here is what was not expected: I found that whenever people were exerting effort, their pupils shrunk and the light in their eyes became dull. It was as if "trying hard" induced tunnel vision and murkiness. When their efforts stopped, suddenly their pupils expanded and filled with light. It was dramatic, and it happened instantaneously because the pupil also responds to any sensory, emotional, or mental change occurring in the autonomic nervous system.

Having had difficulties with reading my entire life and continually being told to "try harder," this discovery helped me see that we are designed to function with little or no effort. I was beginning to realize that our potential as human beings hinged on the subtle balance between striving and thriving. The photos below, taken within seconds of each other, illustrate the real-time changes observed in one child's eyes.

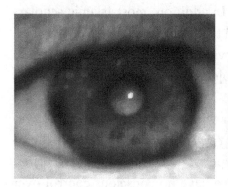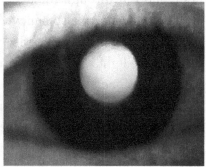

Pupillary reflex during retinoscopy illustrates the difference between exertion and ease

Perhaps this is why the German word for eyesight is *Augenlicht* — literally, "eye light" — and why in Greek, the expressions "I'm losing my light" and "I'm losing my sight" are synonymous.

Having had the opportunity to work with that six-year-old girl allowed me to discover that a person's emotional state is intricately linked to their eyes. Good feelings cause pupils to expand, allowing a greater amount of light to enter and exit the eyes. The light expands our view, allowing our brains to receive and absorb more information. In other words, happiness allows us to see, remember, and understand more, expanding the size of the window through which we see the world.

When a patient's view of life is bleak, their field of vision reflects it and is often reduced to tunnel vision, collapsing their awareness and their ability to perceive and respond to life. Perhaps that's why the ancient Chinese philosopher Lao Tzu said, "Use the light that dwells within you to regain your natural clarity of sight."

As it turns out, the pupil is the body's most sensitive barometer of activity in the autonomic nervous system, responding as much to light entering the eyes as it does to light exiting the eyes. But this is not a new idea. In the second century CE, the renowned Greek philosopher and physician Galen said that vision comes from the brain and out through the eyes. In addition, most Islamic scholars in the ninth century also believed that light emanates from the eyes. Perhaps the pupil is indeed the "window of the soul" in that it both receives the light without and projects the light within — the alignment I mentioned earlier.

Since pupillary changes occur without our knowledge, they reveal our deepest feelings. In *The Human Animal*, zoologist, ethologist, and human sociobiology expert Dr. Desmond Morris writes, "The pupils cannot lie because we have no conscious control over them." This is why professional poker players frequently wear sunglasses while playing; they do not want to reveal how they feel about their cards.

The eyes not only reflect our innermost terrain, but they also reveal when we are truly connecting with another. In fact, Dr. Morris confirms that during "early stages of courtship the eyes transmit vital signals. Since the pupils expand slightly more than usual when they see something they like, we can tell whether we are 'being liked' or not....If, on the other hand, the pupils shrink to pinpricks when we gaze closely at our companion's face, we might as well give up."

In a recent study published in the *Journal of Experimental Psychology: General*, researchers found that when we are deeply involved in speaking and listening to each other our pupillary dilations synchronize, as if our two minds become one.

Such findings fueled my early work, confirming that our eyes dynamically reflect our physical, emotional, and spiritual development more vividly than any other part of the body. This was an epiphany for me because, aside from my experience with Dr. Streff, I had been taught that light's interaction with the eyes was strictly a one-way street. As noted, a number of ancient philosophers, including Plato, Euclid, and Ptolemy, believed that light emanates from the eyes, rendering sight *as much a projective process as a receptive one*.

Trusting Life's Guidance

The ease with which light traverses the human energy system is an indication of how much we trust our life's guidance. If we trust life, we live in a state of effortless flow and our eyes and aura appear bright because no light is lost. If we do not trust life, however, we think ahead and try hard, losing the light naturally visible in our eyes. The light in our eyes is a reflection of our light content, a gauge of our congruence and coherence with life, which is a reflection of our state of consciousness. When our eyes appear dull or dim, they indicate a state of heaviness, stagnation, and a lack of life force. When our eyes appear bright, they indicate grace, flow, and vibrancy.

I also observed that our degree of connectedness with life is reflected in our breathing cycle. When our eyes are bright, our breathing is full and vice versa. Since breathing is one of the most fundamental indicators of physiological coherence, as well as a reflection of the rhythmic expansion and contraction associated with the very cadence of life, it would make sense that an inhibition of this flow would impact us on many levels. Yet most of us respire in a shallow, irregular manner. In his book *Pathways to Peace*, Swami Satchidananda confirms this fact when he asserts, "we use only one-seventh of our lungs in normal breathing."

When I observed how thinking caused my patients to hold their breath, and that it reduced the light emanating from their eyes, I wondered why. I remembered being taught to "work hard" and "try my best" in school, neither of which led to my ultimate success. I eventually realized that working hard might not be the key to our creative breakthroughs, and that "thinking ahead" is often an attempt to combat our fear of the unknown, which can obscure the very answers we seek. Infants and young children do not "think ahead" or look for anything. In fact, they respond to whatever calls their attention, guided by a flow of knowledge available to us all.

So I began to encourage patients' awareness of the subtle machinations they performed while facing tasks they deemed difficult. I helped them shine an inner light on the thoughts and concerns that arose, the strategies they employed to "succeed," and most importantly, whether those strategies worked or not. In the process, they directly experienced how thinking ahead actually kept them behind.

For one of the exercises, I adapted a technique introduced to me by my dear friend and colleague Dr. Ray Gottlieb and originally developed by Dr. Robert Pepper as part of Pepper Stress Therapy. Using a chart with several rows of arrows, each pointing in a different direction, I asked patients to call out the direction of each arrow while simultaneously moving their arms in the *opposite direction* of what the arrow indicated. As you can imagine, this resulted in confusion (if not panic) — and the desire to "get it right" along with the tendency for them to hold their breath. However, when they discovered this and started breathing again, their brilliance emerged free of charge.

I remember a young woman who attended one of my workshops. I asked her to remove her thick glasses and stand as close to the arrow chart as she needed to see it clearly. Since the arrows were fairly large, she was able to see them from about three feet away. Every time she mastered an exercise, I asked her to take a deep breath and step a bit farther from the chart. Within twenty minutes she was twenty-five feet away and still able to see it clearly. I checked her eyesight after that experience and it had improved by 200 percent.

I have since used this exercise and others like it with thousands of individuals, including members of the US Olympic Team and world-class athletes. Time and time again it has led to significant improvements in attention, memory coordination, and sports performance, as well as speed, accuracy, and fluidity of response to complex situations. Most interesting was my observation that our systems seem naturally equipped to respond to life rather than direct it. This became the thrust of my later philosophical inquiry.

We excel when we stop thinking and start responding. When we try to anticipate and control what happens to us rather than responding to life as it presents itself, we tighten up and our performance drops. However, when we flow with life, following wherever it leads us, we meet life head-on with our eyes open. This experience allows us to discover a new level of ease and presence without any effort. Acknowledging that the intelligence of life always has the first move inspires an organic and balanced form of collaboration, as we follow life's invitation toward our greatest potential.

The following story tells of my own "invitation" to explore my potential. In the spring of 1969 I was accepted to dental school under the condition that I complete three summer courses prior to fall enrollment. I contacted the only accredited university in Miami (where I would be spending the summer) and learned that two of the courses were being offered simultaneously, making it impossible to fulfill all three prerequisites before fall enrollment. This meant I would need to wait another year before starting school.

That afternoon, one of my fraternity brothers told me he was going to Memphis to visit his family and asked if I wanted to join. I said yes. After we arrived, my friend took me sightseeing. As we drove down one of the main roads, we passed a college of optometry and I felt compelled to stop there — odd, since I had never considered optometry as a career. "Turn around!" I yelled. He pulled over and I literally ran to the admissions office to ask for an application. Since most of the staff and students were on holiday break, the office was not busy and I received an appointment with the head of admissions the following day.

I told the admissions officer how something inspired me to stop as I passed their campus. I showed him my letter of acceptance to dental school and asked how their course requirements compared. He said they were almost identical and that there was only one space left in their upcoming class; he asked if I wanted to apply. I pulled out the application that I had completed the night before, along with my transcripts. He reviewed them and looked up with a surprised expression. "I've never done this before, but if you want the slot, it's yours!" He then indicated that I was only required to pass *two* of the three science courses required by dental school.

By the time I returned to the University of Georgia the following week a conditional letter of acceptance was waiting for me. I passed the two courses at the University of Miami that summer and began studies at Southern College of Optometry in the fall of 1969.

Foresight Is 20/20

Many years ago while observing an artist at work, I noticed he periodically stepped back and gazed at his canvas. I asked him what he was looking at. He told me he was not aware of looking at anything specifically but just stood back to see if anything seemed incomplete. As he stood there I noticed that his eyes were randomly scanning and only paused when something called their attention. It soon became clear that the artist's eyes showed him where more attention was needed on the canvas, in the same way our eyes are drawn to whatever requires our presence in any given moment.

Our eyes are continually responding to the light that catches them. As we discover this subtle yet profound aspect of our makeup, we begin to trust its guidance and follow it without question, heightening our ability to see the inner workings of our lives with greater clarity and acceptance.

During the separation period prior to my divorce in the late 1970s, my life consisted of a series of extremely upsetting events. I kept having recurring confrontations and reacting to them with angry outbursts. One day, after one of these experiences, I recognized why this pattern was repeating itself in my life. After that, the lag time between one of these incidents and my awareness of why it was happening shortened. I realized that consciousness evolves and, at times, I was able to recognize what was happening as it occurred. Immediately I thought, "Aha! I've finally arrived!" — but as soon as my ego wanted to take credit, I ended up right back at square one.

After a while, however, I had a magical experience. In the midst of a situation that previously would have disturbed me I felt calm and fully aware. I felt a deep sense of humility, as if I were in a state of grace. Shortly after that experience I was once again stopped in my tracks. An event would occur and I would immediately realize that I had sensed it happening just a few minutes earlier. Was this merely a coincidence or can awareness precede experience? Is it possible that we are inseparably connected with the intelligence of life, guided by a form of precognition?

Before giant waves slammed into Sri Lanka and India's coastlines in December 2004, wild and domestic animals seemed to know what was about to happen and started shrieking and fleeing to safety. As a result, very few animals died when the waves hit — yet more than 150,000 people were killed.

As mentioned in the previous chapter, experts believe that animals possess a sixth sense that enables them to recognize imminent danger long before humans do. But humans also possess this sixth sense. The only difference is that we have been taught to question what we instinctively "know" and to trust what we "think." We believe "hindsight is 20/20" because most of us become aware of things after they occur. But what if we are designed to perceive things before they occur? What if foresight is actually 20/20? In Jungian psychology, intuition is the psychological function that allows us to sense what will occur before it happens. Many artists are "ahead of their time," trusting their intuition to guide their visionary work.

Seeing the Invisible

In 2010 I was elected president of the International Society for the Study of Subtle Energies and Energy Medicine (ISSSEEM), an organization of scientists, physicians, and wellness practitioners interested in the impact of consciousness on health and well-being. Three weeks after our annual conference, I had an extraordinary experience.

After falling into a deep sleep one night, I became aware that I was observing myself sleeping in bed. I noticed the rise and fall of my chest and the sounds of my breath. I was also cognizant that my sleeping body was dreaming, as I was able to see the dream.

In the dream, two people were introducing me to a large audience at the 2011 ISSSEEM conference — one was my daughter and the other a close friend. I then proceeded to deliver the presidential address, after which I received a standing ovation.

A couple months after the dream my daughter called and asked if I thought her partner at the time could submit a proposal to speak at the 2011 conference. I agreed, but since he led safaris in Africa I could not imagine what he would present that would be pertinent to the focus of the group.

In early October the Program Committee met in California to finalize their list of presenters. When we began discussing applicants, my colleagues were excited about a proposal from this fellow who wanted to discuss conscious human contact with animals in the African wild. I listened quietly. Within minutes the committee had agreed to invite him to speak. I had never told them that he was my daughter's boyfriend.

As it turned out, my daughter attended the 2011 conference with her partner. When a former ISSSEEM president who was slated to introduce me became ill at the last moment, my daughter and close friend Brian ended up doing it, and following my presentation there was indeed an ovation. I had not been dreaming after all.

This experience was fascinating for many reasons, including the fact that everything I had previously learned about sleep described deep, dreamless sleep as unconsciousness. Yet consciousness was obviously awake and aware, pointing to the ever-present nature of awareness.

As an example, a 2013 study published in the journal *PLOS ONE* found that experienced meditators who claim to be aware during deep sleep exhibit brain activity typically seen during waking consciousness. To further confirm this, a recent meta-analysis published in the December 2016 issue of *Trends in Cognitive Sciences* suggests that consciousness does not turn off when one enters deep sleep. According to Evan Thompson, professor at the University of British Columbia and one of the paper's authors, "Consciousness, in the sense of sheer awareness or feeling of being or existing, continues in deep sleep, even when ordinary mental activity (thoughts, emotions, mental images) has quieted down or stopped." The evidence presented in these studies along with my direct experience led me to believe that, like light, consciousness is all-pervasive.

An Ocean in a Drop

Years ago while spiritual teacher Ram Dass was visiting Maui, I invited him to sit in with a men's group I had been part of for many years. During our sharing, one of the members asked Ram Dass to speak about presence.

"Presence," he said, "is like baklava — it includes everything... the nuts, the honey, the phyllo dough."

It was a funny way to describe presence. Yet it was so true. Presence is pure awareness and includes everything, even those times we do not think we are being present. Most of us think of being present in relation to others, our feelings, or a specific situation. But that is based on the idea that we are living life separately from one another rather than recognizing that *we are life*, inextricably linked to every living thing.

In any given moment everything and everyone is intimately connected to and collaborating with everything else. The same force that moves the tides and changes the seasons also animates the beating of our heart. So when an insight or a feeling suddenly imprints on our awareness, it is not an accident. The intelligence of life is looking for us, effortlessly directing us toward the next step on our journey. There is nothing to think about, consider, or choose. Just observe, and we will be guided to where we need to be and what we need to do.

Awareness and experience are seamlessly linked. When that becomes clear, the *drop* that we think of as our individual self merges with the *ocean* of oneness, creating waves of *presence* that expand infinitely in all directions. When the light within us merges with the light illuminating our awareness, we are effortlessly moved toward our source, in the same way that a flower is moved toward the sun.

CHAPTER THREE

Living on Light

All the energy which we take into our bodies is derived from the sun.
— ALBERT SZENT-GYORGYI

In 1896 Wilbur Atwater and Francis Benedict conducted a series of metabolic experiments that suggested that the human body's production of heat and physiological activities corresponded to the caloric value of the nutrients ingested. Their findings became the basis of the calorie theory.

Based on Atwater's findings, Francis Benedict and James Harris developed the Harris-Benedict equation in 1919, making it possible to determine one's basal metabolic rate or how many calories the human body requires at rest.

This theory stood unchallenged for over fifty years. Then, beginning in 1972, a team of research scientists headed by Dr. Paul Webb conducted a series of studies using state-of-the-art technology in an attempt to replicate Atwater and Benedict's results. Webb's findings, published in the *American Journal of Clinical Nutrition*, uncovered a significant discrepancy between the theoretical amounts of energy produced by metabolism versus the actual amount of energy produced by the body. This difference, referred to as "unmeasured energy," indicates that as much as 23 percent of the energy produced by the human body could not be attributed to one's caloric intake.

To further corroborate his discoveries, Webb reviewed all scientific studies related to the subject and found that they not only confirmed his findings but also demonstrated that the more precise the study, the clearer the evidence that a significant amount of energy could not be scientifically explained.

Confronted with the fact that there was energy that could not be accounted for, Webb introduced a new variable that he referred to as Qx into the calculation of energy balance. This variable represented energy that originated from an unknown source, or energy derived from what some call *nothingness*.

Although the idea of energy derived from "nothingness" may seem strange from a Western perspective, Eastern cultures have been aware of this mysterious life-force energy for thousands of years. In China it is called *chi*, in India *prana*, and renowned Austrian psychoanalyst Wilhelm Reich referred to it as *orgone*.

Webb's research not only exposed the shortcomings of the calorie theory but also demonstrated that the human body receives energy (or life force) from an unknown source. The research also discovered that the greater the food deficit, the larger the unmeasured energy. In other words, the body appears to receive a significant amount of energy from an unknown source, and the less we eat the more energy it receives.

Webb's discovery seems to be verified by the case of yogi Prahlad Jani, who claims to have lived without food or water since 1940. Although this sounds unbelievable, this Indian yogi was evaluated twice under the most stringent of controlled scientific conditions, and each time he was deemed physiologically normal.

In 2003 Prahlad Jani first underwent a rigorous ten-day evaluation at Sterling Hospital in Ahmedabad, India. During the study Jani was evaluated by dozens of medical experts, and all pertinent tests, including daily blood cell counts and CT scans of the body, were administered. In addition, he was under around-the-clock surveillance in a locked room with no access to food or water; the bathroom was sealed off, his clothes and sheets were scrutinized for any traces of urine, and mobile cameras filmed him whenever clinic personnel escorted him from his locked room to an office or laboratory for medical evaluation.

Dr. Urman Dhruv, who supervised and approved the study protocol, stated that Jani did not consume anything orally, including fluids of any type or food during the ten-day study. He also did not pass any urine or stool during that period. In the words of Dr. Sudhir Shah, the initiator of the study, "We are all scientifically educated and research-orientated doctors....And our entire knowledge has been shaken to the core."

Under ideal circumstances, it is conceivable that humans can live ten to fifteen days without drinking. However, after four to six days without eating, drinking, and urinating, one would expect extremely high levels of uremic waste products. Nevertheless, Jani's blood and metabolic levels remained in the safe range during the entire project!

In 2010 Jani was once again rigorously evaluated for fifteen days at Sterling Hospital. This time, a team of thirty-five researchers from the Indian Defense Institute of Physiology and Allied Sciences (DIPAS) studied him. After fifteen days of not eating, drinking, urinating, or defecating, all medical tests on Jani were reported as normal, and researchers said that Jani was in better health than someone half his age. Representatives from DIPAS stated in 2010 that further studies were planned to investigate, among other things, where Jani's body derives its energy for sustenance.

In the February 9, 1901, issue of *Collier's Weekly*, Nikola Tesla wrote, "Why should a living being not be able to obtain all the energy it needs for the performance of its life functions from the environment, instead of through consumption of food?" Today, Dr. Gerald H. Pollack, professor of bioengineering at the University of Washington and author of *The Fourth Phase of Water*, may be able to demonstrate how that process actually occurs.

Living Water

According to Pollack, "Experimental evidence shows that light imparts energy to water, including body water. That energy may, in some instances, provide enough energy for sustaining life." Pollack and his team have confirmed that there exists a fourth phase of water, beyond that of solid, liquid, and gas. The body's cells are composed of this "living water," which differs from normal water, as it is imbued with light.

Fourth-phase water, H_3O_2, is more viscous, dense, organized, and alkaline than H_2O and has more available oxygen due to its chemical structure. It has a negative charge and, like a battery, can store the energy contained in sunlight and deliver it as needed. Since the energy required for structuring water comes from the sun, you might say that the body is a biological photocell filled with "living water" that is constantly charged by the sun.

In spite of the stringent medical assessment and scientific scrutiny that Prahlad Jani underwent, the current scientific findings of Pollack, and the powerful documentary by P. A. Straubinger titled *In the Beginning There Was Light*, most doctors and scientists still do not consider the possibility that our bodies may actually run on sunlight.

The Power of Light

Earlier I mentioned that Nobel laureate Albert Szent-Gyorgyi said that "all the energy which we take into our bodies is derived from the sun." The sun's energy, through the process of photosynthesis, is stored in plants, which are then eaten by animals and humans, who use this light-created energy. But is it possible that we can supplement this process even further by spending more time outdoors in natural light? If solar power can run our homes, cars, and cities, is it so far-fetched to consider that sunlight may also be powering our lives?

According to physician and photobiologist Alexander Wunsch, only one-third of the energy produced by our body comes from the food we eat. The balance comes from the light we are exposed to. In essence, the body's energy production involves a lot more than just eating right. The body is always seeking homeostasis, and most of the energy required to maintain that essential balance comes from the sunlight we ingest. The easiest way to get our minimum daily requirement of sunlight is to spend some time outdoors each day, revealing as much of our skin as possible. The body is powered by both food and light. That is why sunlight — *nature's optimal fuel mix for life* — is so critical for our health and well-being.

Perhaps this is why fasting, accompanied by sunbathing, has been used for centuries across cultures for spiritual and physical cleansing, renewal, and replenishment. It can help us recover from illness and injury and has been shown effective in the prevention and treatment of numerous chronic health conditions. Could the process of eating less and spending more time in nature impact our health and wellness in ways we may have not considered?

Although the information in this chapter about living on light is fascinating, I am not suggesting anyone should stop eating, as I myself love to eat. However, I think it is important that we consider the significance of light as not only a guide for our eyes but also for our entire physiology and journey through life. This *light* guidance, received through the gateway of *presence*, is not only directing every aspect of our lives but is also nourishing us at levels we cannot even imagine.

The nutritional value of our food is related to its light content. Organically grown fruits and vegetables that are harvested when ripe and eaten fresh are light-filled and nutritionally rich. Now consider the health benefits of eating less, spending more time outdoors each day, and receiving the ultrapure nourishment of light directly rather than receiving it indirectly via food.

Eating a simpler, lighter diet has been shown to promote healthier aging by shielding the body's cells from deterioration and other major health risks. In addition, it has been confirmed that underfed lab animals live longer, healthier lives and rarely develop age-related pathologies such as cancer and heart disease. According to evolutionary biologist Dr. Margo Adler of the University of New South Wales in Australia, "cutting back on food leads to increased rates of 'cellular recycling' and repair mechanisms in the body." Perhaps this is why Prahlad Jani was reported by researchers to be in better health than someone half his age.

Jani's extraordinary state of health was not just related to the fact that he did not eat or drink. He also received great health benefits from sunbathing, as spending time outdoors stimulates the production of vitamin D. The significance of this is paramount, as vitamin D deficiency, which is associated with not spending enough time in sunlight, has become a modern-day epidemic, strongly linked to a rise in the incidence of the "diseases of civilization" such as cancer, heart disease, osteoporosis, macular degeneration, and immune deficiencies. Scientists have also confirmed a significant relationship between sunlight-related vitamin D deficiency and the development of dementia and Alzheimer's disease.

As you can see, sunlight profoundly influences every facet of our lives, from our overall health and well-being to the quality and efficiency of our vision. These astonishing discoveries about light, paired with the instantaneous healing of my vision and clinical experience with light therapy, sparked the curiosity of those I worked with, opening them to new possibilities within themselves. I had been trained to believe that disease was contagious, but wellness is even more contagious — and the potential for recovery in my patients increased *in direct proportion to the space I was able to hold for what was possible.*

Wellness Is Contagious

Over the years, many people have contacted me after my lectures to say that their vision had improved, or they stopped wearing glasses altogether, just by being open to the possibility. Many of them have kept in touch, including a woman who wrote this after attending a presentation on light: "You are responsible for a spontaneous remission of poor vision. After listening to your words, I could see without my glasses."

I heard from another patient recently whom I had treated as a child, who is now a successful actress with a child of her own:

> I remember being excited about going to the doctor's office. I was only five or six, but remember jumping on the trampoline and the sugar-free lollipops. Most importantly, I remember the day Dr. Liberman took the glasses off my face and told me I didn't need them anymore. I remember always wearing glasses as a kid until the day he told me I didn't need them anymore. And I never needed them since. Even though my family's eyesight is terrible, I've always had 20/20 vision.

Growing up with parents who were diagnosed with multiple cancers instilled me with a fear that haunted me for much of my life. They both survived, but the fear of the cancer's recurrence left a permanent mark on our family. I realized that it is often not the disease that kills us but the diagnosis. Many people rid their body of cancer, but few can rid their mind of it.

When I went into practice I noticed this same phenomenon with patients who came to me with diagnoses of learning problems such as attention deficit disorder (ADD) or dyslexia. We could often resolve their issue, but once they had been labeled, the diagnosis remained part of their identity. Here is a true personal story that illustrates that point.

One Saturday afternoon while flossing my teeth, I noticed what appeared to be a brown growth in the back of my throat that I had never seen before. My mind instantly went back to when my father was diagnosed with a cancerous growth in his throat. I kept checking my throat, and every time I looked the brown growth seemed larger. My heart was pounding, my forehead was drenched in sweat, and I was chilled.

A moment before, I was feeling wonderful and now I felt as if I was dying. I thought about going to the hospital, but feared that I might receive a fatal diagnosis, and everything I had worked for would have been for nothing. After dwelling on this for a while I picked up the phone and called a doctor friend.

He asked, "What's wrong?"

"Victor, I'm terrified. Both of my parents had cancer when I was a kid."

"I don't understand — what's the problem?"

"My parents are both alive and healthy now, but cancer has always been scary for me because we never spoke about it openly."

"I still don't understand what's wrong."

"Well, I looked in the mirror this afternoon and there was a brown growth in the back of my throat. It looks like a mole or something."

He asked me a few more questions then told me to feel the bump with my finger. When I finally managed to squeeze my hand into the back of my mouth, I pulled something out. On the tip of my finger was a small piece of the chocolate macaroon I had eaten for lunch!

Health-care practitioners must find new ways of seeing and discussing the ailments their patients are dealing with. The practice of diagnostic labeling often frightens the patient and limits both the doctor's belief in a patient's ability to recover as well as the patient's faith in their own ability to heal. Our ideas and beliefs about life limit our ability to experience it fully. Having expanded my own views of what is possible allowed me to experience our extraordinary capacity for healing and living at our highest potential, which emerges naturally when we trust in the intelligence of life.

CHAPTER FOUR

The Intelligence of Life

Everything is determined, the beginning as well as the end, by forces over which we have no control. It is determined for the insect, as well as for the star. Human beings, vegetables, or cosmic dust, we all dance to a mysterious tune, intoned in the distance by an invisible piper.

— ALBERT EINSTEIN

In 2012 I was invited to be a speaker at the first TEDx conference on Maui. As I sat in the audience listening to the other speakers, one of them, author and scientist Dr. Gary Greenberg, said something that caught my attention: "Every cell has a job."

As I sat with that statement I realized how profound it was. Cardiac cells pump blood, red blood cells deliver oxygen, white blood cells fight infection, fat cells store excess energy, and immune cells attack foreign organisms. What struck me deeply was the recognition that each of us, like these cells, also has a job to fulfill.

I have often said that we are each like different kinds of trees. Some trees are tall, thin, and sway easily, while others have thicker trunks and less elasticity. Some trees are inviting because they bear fruit or flowers, while others encourage caution with their protective thorns. Like trees, we are all different and serve a unique function in maintaining the fullness and balance of life. As the great Indian sage Ramana Maharshi said, "One comes into existence for a certain purpose." And the intelligence of life is constantly keeping us on course.

Visionaries throughout history seem to agree that the universe is continuously activating and regulating itself in accordance with some unseen harmony, and we are an intricate part of that dance. According to the philosophy of Stoicism, established by Zeno of Citium in the fourth century BCE, "The entire cosmos is organized by an ordering force.... The human being also contains such an organizing or guiding element."

Echoing this ancient philosophy, Mahatma Gandhi writes, "There is a force in the universe, which, if we permit it, will flow through us and produce miraculous results."

Our lives are animated and guided by the same force that moves the planets in our solar system through their orbit. I now know that my life's purpose is to help others *see*. The intelligence of life helped me realize this by creating experiences from the time of my birth that supported me in discovering who I am and what I am here to share. It all began with my name.

Judaism places great importance on naming a child, as it is believed that a persons's name represents their connection both to previous generations and to their destiny. Among Eastern European Jews, it is customary to name a child after a deceased relative as a way of honoring the ancestor as well as perpetuating their essence. My birth name, Jacob Israel Liberman, is the same as my grandfather's. I am the son of Joseph Chaim Liberman and a descendant of the tribe of Levi, or the Levites (spiritual leaders designated for divine service). As I have journeyed through life I have learned that "Jacob Israel" accurately describes who I am, my life's experiences, and my purpose for being.

I could not relate to my birth name early in life, and then in 1988, at the age of forty, I had an epiphany while attending a lecture about biblical prophets and how they dealt with hard times. The psychiatrist speaking said that after the prophet Jacob wrestled a man with preternatural strength, he was dubbed "Israel," because he had struggled with both man and God and had prevailed. Having gone through a devastating divorce, followed by six years of severe panic attacks, I could definitely relate to the "Jacob" he described.

While teaching in Israel in 1992 I had an experience that further illuminated the relationship between my name and my destiny. One evening, while I was being driven to the city of Tzfat, my hosts got lost. As they pulled over to look at a map, a sliver of light appeared from behind the door of a nearby house. We knocked in hopes of getting directions. A man with long gray hair and a beard answered. My host introduced himself and his wife, and then told the man that I was visiting from the United States and that my name was Jacob Israel. The man looked deep into my eyes and said, "I have been waiting for you," and invited us in.

For the next few hours he explained that in Jewish mysticism the Tree of Life is the central symbol of the esoteric teachings of Kabbalah, and that the prophet Jacob occupies the most central position on the tree — integrating qualities of giving and receiving with heaven and earth. "*Jacob*," he said, "means heel of the foot, or connection with the earth. *Israel* means top of the head, or connection with the heavens. In other words, *Israel* means to be aligned with God.

"When Jacob became Israel," he said, "that was the moment of his enlightenment. He realized that by keeping a direct connection with the Divine, his path would always be illuminated." He then presented me with a beautiful Star of David that he said he had made for me, even though we had just met. Later that evening I remembered my father always advising me to "travel the straight road." I wondered if that was his way of reminding me to always remain true to my highest calling.

Another example of how my life's journey helped me *see* what my unique contribution was meant to be involved the miraculous healing of my vision in 1976. During my daily meditation, which I had been practicing for a few years, I experienced seeing in a way that I could not understand or describe at the time. My eyes were closed, but *I* could see the entire room, including myself, with total, almost shimmering, clarity. It felt as if I were an infinite field of eyes seeing from all vantage points simultaneously. This was not just optical clarity; there was also a deep awareness present, devoid of all questions and answers — a sense of *knowing*, without a *knower*. I felt as though *I had become the sky*.

When I opened my eyes I could see perfectly. So I drove to my office to check my eyes. My eyesight had improved *300 percent*, yet the optical measurements of my eyes had not changed at all. To this day I still do not know how it happened. Yet somehow I experienced effortless seeing from a source *beyond my eyes*, with no point of view. I then stopped "looking" and started "seeing" what was beyond mere sight and began to correlate those discoveries to share with others. Although that revelation occurred forty years ago, I can still see well without glasses, and I am still sharing my insights about seeing, being, and living. This is my life's work, what I love to do — my reason for being.

How We Receive the Intelligence of Life

The Bible states that God is light (1 John 1:5). God, who is omnipotent (Job 9:4–10), omniscient (Psalm 147:5), and omnipresent (Psalm 139:7–10), created the heavens and the earth (Genesis 1:1) and created human beings in the divine image (Genesis 1:27). What is fascinating about the biblical descriptions of God is that quantum physicists, using different terms, describe light in the same way. They state that light is the foundation of everything that exists, and behaves as if it is omnipotent, omniscient, and omnipresent. In essence, everything we experience in life as matter is the formed expression of a formless essence called light, and human beings are holographic focal points of that light.

When the light of God (the invisible light physicists refer to as the ground of reality) interacts and merges with our "inner light" —

the light of consciousness — we are instantaneously activated into a receptive state called *presence*, or coherent guidance, which naturally provides the next step in our life's journey.

This "inner light" is not only a universal metaphor for health and awareness but also a quantifiable phenomenon. It is well documented that all living organisms, including humans, emit a measurable low-intensity glow known as biophoton emission that reflects one's state of wellness or illness before every biochemical reaction. Without this emission of "inner light," the intra- and intercellular communications and the biochemical reactions they catalyze to keep our life in balance would not occur. The greater the degree of cellular and organismic harmony, the more the body, like a battery, holds on to its light energy and the lower the biophoton emission.

In addition to the biophoton emission released by all living organisms, more than half of all marine organisms — from plankton to sharks — and up to 80 percent of ray-finned fishes make their own light to lure prey, discourage predators, attract mates, and communicate. For example, scientists from the American Museum of Natural History recently discovered that certain creatures absorb light and then reemit it as a different color. According to researchers, the "glow" produced by this reemitted light, called biofluorescence, increases in contrast so that fish can communicate with one another.

Humans also absorb light and reemit it as different colors in their biofield or aura, which appears as a subtle fluorescent or iridescent luminous field surrounding a person. Based on my many years of observing this phenomenon, it appears that the light we absorb and the light we reradiate reflects our physical, mental, emotional, and spiritual state of wellness. Our beliefs and the emotions associated with them affect the way we relate to the light spectrum, coloring both our world and our aura. However, most of us do not notice this subtle indicator of one's state of being because, for most of us, our natural ability to see auras is undeveloped.

Since the human body consists of approximately thirty-seven trillion cells, which are constantly communicating and collaborating with each other at unimaginable speeds, a cell's ability to literally "see" the intelligence encoded in light is crucial to every aspect of our health and wellness.

This ability is of obvious importance in complex biological processes such as photosynthesis in plants, or when a photon of light interacts with the eye, initiating the process of vision. But new research, published in the journal *Science*, has captured the most detailed picture to date of the almost instantaneous process by which a photosensitive protein in purple bacteria responds to light's guidance by acting as an "eye."

Using the world's most powerful x-ray laser, along with the world's fastest camera, German scientist and professor Marius Schmidt and his colleagues, along with researchers from the SLAC National Accelerator Laboratory, captured the subtle changes in the configuration of a photosensitive yellow protein occurring as fast as one hundred quadrillionths of a second. That is a thousand times faster than earlier results.

This important discovery reveals how this initial response to light creates a domino effect in the protein, setting the stage for its biological function. Prior to these findings, researchers had never observed the crucial details of how biomolecules respond to light.

The immediate way our cells respond to light is only the beginning of this miraculous discovery. Because we are each a cell within the organism called the universe, we are designed to infinitely communicate and cooperate with one another. This process reveals that we live in a relational universe where everything is intimately connected with everything else.

Heart to Heart

Modern science has confirmed that, at a fundamental level, we are inseparable; we are facets of the same organism continually affecting and being affected by each other. As German writer and politician Johann Wolfgang von Goethe writes, "So divinely is the world organized that every one of us, in our place and time, is in balance with everything else." According to theoretical physicist David Bohm, "Everything is connected to everything else, and affected [instantaneously] by everything that happens to everything else." In essence, relationship is the most fundamental aspect of existence.

In his book *The Hidden Life of Trees*, Peter Wohlleben describes "trees in the forest [as] social beings. They can count, learn, and remember; nurse sick neighbors; warn each other of danger…and, for reasons unknown, keep the ancient stumps of long-felled companions alive for centuries by feeding them a sugar solution through their roots. Sometimes, pairs…are so interconnected at the roots that when one tree dies, the other one dies, too."

In humans, the ability to meaningfully connect with others is primarily a function of the heart. We often speak of this ability as having a heart-to-heart connection.

Scientists have long believed that the brain is the conductor of the body's symphony, instructing the body on what to do, when to do it, and to what degree. But research conducted at the Institute of HeartMath has demonstrated not only that the heart sends more signals to the brain than the brain sends to the heart, but that these heart-generated signals significantly affect brain function. The heart generates the body's most powerful and extensive electromagnetic field, sixty times greater in amplitude than that of the brain. In addition, the heart's magnetic field is five thousand times stronger than the brain's and can be detected several feet away from the body.

This makes sense when you consider that the heart reflects our emotional state, entraining our physiology as well as the physiology of those around us. When we are feeling love, intimacy, gratitude, or appreciation, our heart creates a contagious frequency of harmony. But when our life is in an uproar, our heart rhythm pattern reflects that as well, giving new meaning to the expression "speaking from the heart."

In his book *Love and Survival: The Scientific Basis for the Healing Power of Intimacy*, Dr. Dean Ornish writes, "I am not aware of any other factor in medicine — not diet, not smoking, not exercise, not stress, not genetics, not drugs, not surgery — that has a greater impact on our quality of life, incidence of illness, and premature death from all causes than love and intimacy." The love and intimacy Ornish describes is a yearning for oneness that is inherent to the matrix of life.

Everything in the universe has a reason for being and is inseparably connected and directed by the same intelligence. When we recognize that our bond is the source of our individual and collective potential, we breathe easier, feel a deep sense of relief, and experience the unconditional love and intimacy that bind us.

Seeing with Our Hearts

Over my many years of training physicians and others in the healthcare field, I have always said, "Don't work with anyone you don't love." The reason is simple: the relationship between the individual offering assistance and the one receiving it is the most potent aspect of the healing process. When we experience authentic love and caring we naturally relax and trust that we are *in good hands*. It is the power of that connection that melts our fears, helping us see a problem as a *blessing in disguise*.

I had the pleasure of working with a young woman who allowed me to symbolically hold her hand as she gradually transformed a crisis into an opportunity, unearthing the profound healing power of love and intimacy.

In 2012 I was contacted by the mother of a sixteen-year-old undergoing a health crisis. Her daughter had experienced a series of bad headaches over a couple of days, followed by dizzy spells, nausea, and an acute loss of vision. Her mother took her to a physician, then to an optometrist who did a series of tests but could find nothing wrong. The girl was referred to an ophthalmologist and then a neurologist who ordered a CT scan, an MRI, and some blood tests. The results were all negative. A chiropractor and craniosacral therapist also treated her, but nothing changed. By then the girl had grown concerned because she was otherwise quite healthy and had not been under an inordinate amount of stress; every doctor said she should be seeing fine — but she was not.

During our first meeting I checked the young woman's visual acuity and found that she was legally blind; she was only able to see the big *E* on the eye chart. As she described her symptoms, I had an intuition that there was something significant about the year 2006 in her life. While I had no idea where this notion came from or if it was even relevant, I asked if anything traumatic had happened then. Though she could not recall anything herself, her mother said that her daughter's grandmother had died that year. In that moment her tears began to flow and our work together commenced with a gentle light therapy protocol and a very weak (+.50) pair of reading glasses that were meant to "soften the world." Here is her account of our first week of treatment:

> The first time I looked at the turquoise light I started to think about my grandma and cried. I realized that I hadn't really had a chance to cry when she died.... When everyone was saying their goodbyes to Grandma, I often left the room to cry because I didn't want anybody to see me.... That crying continued for the next five days before all the pain, guilt, and feelings I had pushed down were able to finally surface again.

After nine days of light therapy she was seeing 100 percent better. So I suggested she do the treatment twice a day and continue wearing the glasses. She told me that the turquoise light was now her friend because it helped her remember all the things she previously did not want to feel.

She said, "As the emotions came up, sometimes I cried, sometimes I laughed, and sometimes I just looked at the light. If I had a rough day at school I would just let out the feelings I was keeping in. If that light were a person, it would know how I felt about everything."

As she continued the treatment, her vision improved, she felt more relaxed, and was able to more easily express herself. By the time she completed her light therapy her outlook on life had changed. She was seeing 400 percent better, was able to adapt to new situations with greater ease, and no longer felt that it was her responsibility to take care of others. Instead, she now enjoyed making them laugh.

While working with this young woman I recognized how easy it is to discount or override the invisible guidance we receive. In fact, this guidance can, at times, have life-changing effects when shared. When I asked if anything traumatic had happened in 2006, that was not a thought I had but a hint I was given. It opened the door that allowed greater trust for both of us, facilitating a series of events that may have altered the course of this young woman's life.

The Guiding Hand

Our lives grow richer as we focus less on the visible world and more on the invisible one. We become increasingly aware of the *calling* that moves us to look in a certain direction — the lead wave within the ocean of awareness that points our compass toward its next directive. Sometimes we speak of individuals who can tap into this level of seeing as "intuitive" or "psychic," yet we have all had experiences like these.

You are sitting at your desk and suddenly the image of someone flashes into your mind. Without a thought, you pick up the phone, dial their number, and when the person at the other end hears your voice they say, "I was just thinking about you!" Or perhaps your phone rings, and it is the very person you were just sensing, confirming a connection you feel that transcends the boundaries of the rational mind.

In 1986 I had an unusual experience that solidified my sense of our inseparability. I was taking a shower when suddenly I felt a sharp pain in my heart and started sobbing. Immediately I *knew* that Elliot, my dear friend, colleague, and mentor, had died. I stepped out of the shower, soaking wet, walked to the telephone in my bedroom, and dialed his number in New York. His wife answered, at which time I said, "Libby, when did he die?"

She said, "Jacob, how did you know? He passed just moments ago."

So often in life we focus on the things we want to accomplish, missing the subtleties directing our journey. But it is in these "whispers" that the real magic lies. After working with thousands of people, I have come to realize that my job is not necessarily to identify and solve problems but rather to gently recede into the background and allow the intelligence of life to guide the process. Serving as an intermediary between the formless information received and the well-being of the patient, I have come to discover that by doing less, more happens, and by doing nothing, everything happens.

Much like the Taoist concept of *wei wu wei*, which I will discuss in chapter 8, doing "nothing" does not imply that nothing happens. We simply allow something larger to lead, which reinforces our trust in the wisdom of life. Seventeenth-century priest, physician, and mystic Angelus Silesius expressed this concept eloquently when he said, "God, whose love and joy are present everywhere, can't come to visit you unless you aren't there."

Seventeenth-century French playwright Molière said, "If we leave nature alone, she recovers gently from the disorders into which she has fallen. It is our anxiety, our impatience, which spoils all; and nearly all men die of their remedies not of their diseases."

We live in a universe designed to function in the most economical way, whether we are discussing the workings of the body, Mother Nature, or the universe as a whole. That means that life is super-efficient and operates with the least amount of effort. The least amount of effort is the state called *presence*. The healing experiences shared in this chapter illustrate how the power of presence provides each of us the wisdom to be instruments of the Divine.

Wisdom has no author; it moves through us anonymously. The intelligence of life effortlessly directs nature and all its inhabitants. As this guidance moves through us, our personality disappears and what remains is a contagious radiance entraining everything and everyone into a state of wellness.

Spontaneous Healing

Not long ago I was sitting in the steam room of a local spa when I noticed a man walking outside. He was holding on to the wall and walked as if he was visually or physically challenged. He then entered the steam room very carefully, sat down, and introduced himself. After coughing for several minutes he told me that he had a condition similar to multiple sclerosis that significantly affected his gross and fine motor coordination, speech, and most of his internal functions. He also told me that he was a teacher and writer for years prior to receiving the diagnosis of his illness.

He asked me what I did. I told him that I was working on a new book about how life always guides us to do what we know by heart. At that point he began to share passionately about his interests, and as I listened attentively he literally transformed before my eyes. His speech cleared, his balance and coordination normalized, his face appeared less inflamed, and his eyes became clear and sparkly. He was no longer the man I had met just forty-five minutes earlier.

When he finished speaking I told him that he had a great deal of wisdom and needed to teach again. When he shared his passion for what he knew by heart, it was as if his disease had miraculously disappeared.

That is what can happen when our passion is ignited, and we feel unconditional love for one another and for life itself. According to *A Course in Miracles*, "Miracles occur naturally as expressions of love. The real miracle is the love that inspires them. In this sense everything that comes from love is a miracle." In recognizing our life's purpose and inseparable connection with all that exists, we embrace the *great mystery* illuminating our journey, becoming a living expression of *presence* and the love and caring that flows from it.

Up to this point I have shared how the intelligence of life, encoded in light, continually guides our eyes, our physiology, and our lives. It evolves our humanity and instills an ongoing state of contentment. When most people think of light, however, they imagine the illumination created by the sun. But how do we see and how are we guided when the light of the sun is not available? What guides us at night?

CHAPTER FIVE

The Light in Our Dreams

All the things one has forgotten scream for help in dreams.
— ELIAS CANETTI

*H*ave you ever wondered how we see in our dreams when our eyes are closed and there is no light? Or how we can hear, smell, taste, and even touch things? During the night, our dreams contain incredibly vivid images, thoughts, sounds, voices, and subjective sensations that feel so real that upon waking we often think that we have actually experienced them. So what is the difference between how we see during the day and how we see in our dreams?

In his book *Catching the Light: The Entwined History of Light and Mind*, noted physicist Arthur Zajonc details an experiment he conducted called Project Eureka, in which:

> One views a region of space filled with light. It is a simple but startling demonstration that uses only a carefully fabricated box and a powerful projector whose light shines directly into it. We have taken special care to ensure that light does not illuminate any interior objects or surfaces in the box. Within the box, there is only pure light, and lots of it. The question

is: What does one see? How does light look when left entirely to itself?

What would we expect to see upon looking into this contraption? Some evidence of light, of course. But what Zajonc actually saw was "absolute darkness! I see nothing but the blackness of empty space." Zajonc's experiment clearly demonstrates that light is the *invisible* potential that *magically* makes all things *visible*. All that we consider to be visible in our waking lives is actually the result of light interacting with the eye, sparking a release of energy that the conscious mind translates into an image that appears full of light. But the illumination we think is light is only a mental impression, not light itself. So what allows us to see our dreams in the darkness of night when there is no light for the conscious mind to translate into an image?

We know that light directs and illuminates our journey by day. But to answer the question above we must first examine the link between light and consciousness.

In chapter 1 I stated that light and life are the same energy in two different states of existence — form (matter) and formlessness (light). In its formed state, light composes all the matter in the universe. In its formless state, light is a field of pure potentiality. Paramahansa Yogananda, the twentieth-century spiritual leader who introduced many Westerners to meditation, referred to light as "the cosmic intelligent vibration that structures finite creation."

Both light and consciousness are invisible; they are more elementary than time, space, and matter, and fundamental to the universe and our experience of it. Light is the source of the material universe and the messenger of its informational content. Likewise, consciousness is the means by which all sentient beings experience the material universe and extract the wisdom contained within it. Scientists tell us that light interconnects the entire cosmos, and many of our greatest visionaries believe that consciousness is universal.

Dreams are where our fears and concerns about life repeatedly appear in a symbolic manner. This provides us a depth of awareness to help integrate our lives, as facilitated by what twentieth-century psychoanalyst Carl Jung calls the objective psyche or consciousness. If we are fortunate, we might have a lucid dream and realize that we are observing the dream and are in the dream at the same time, as illustrated by the lucid ISSSEEM presidential address dream I shared earlier. With greater lucidity, we may even come to realize that the witness, the individual dreaming, and the dream itself are one.

Recently I mentored a client whose dreams vividly illustrate how the light of consciousness guides us in the darkness of night, illuminating our life's journey, while revealing the true nature of seeing. Although she had worn contact lenses for twenty-five years and could see 20/20, her dreams signaled the beginning of a journey to "see" in a new way — months before she knew that journey was upon her.

After learning that her boyfriend was still emotionally attached to his former girlfriend, she asked for greater transparency in their relationship but he refused. That night she had this dream:

> He and I were in a car, and I was driving us down a dark dirt road without headlights.... Then we came to the "main road" and I saw another car come from my left. The headlights of that car illuminated the road, and I suddenly realized that I couldn't see. I told my boyfriend, "I just realized that I'm not wearing my contacts and can't see very well. I don't feel safe driving."
>
> "Then you shouldn't drive," he said, and got out of the car to take the driver's seat.

"I woke up before he got back into the car," she explained.

"After that dream, I realized that I couldn't see what was really going on in my relationship and that I wanted my partner to take the 'driver's seat,'" she told me.

Concerned about her vision, she reached out to me, initially inquiring about Lasik surgery to "fix" her myopia so she could see without glasses. I explained that her eyes were not the problem and showed her that she could read 20/20 with half her prescription, demonstrating that her eyesight was actually expanding. I suggested a weaker prescription and told her only to wear her glasses when she absolutely needed them. I instructed her to notice any feelings and emotions that she was experiencing when she reached for them.

On a subsequent visit she reported that when she was not wearing her glasses she felt more relaxed, experienced less tension while reading, and stopped cleaning compulsively. I rechecked her and, once again, her eyesight had improved. So I suggested a weaker prescription and asked if she remembered what was happening in her life just prior to getting her first pair of glasses. Immediately she replied, "Yeah, I had run away from home." She then told me her father moved away when she was twelve, catalyzing what felt like a psychological break, followed by a tumultuous period at home. As she began to contemplate the events that took place at that time in her life, she knew it was "the key to understanding more than just my eyes."

As our work progressed her vision continued to improve, and she noticed that she left home on several occasions without putting in her contact lenses. She was breathing easier and allowing the world to come to her rather than reaching out for it. She then realized that her discomfort with not being able to see was a reflection of her uneasiness with feeling vulnerable and being "seen" in that vulnerability. That revelation led to a dream filled with light of an etheric nature, embodying a purity that she described as uplifting, representing in her own words, "a soul quality of seeing." Shortly after that dream her vision once again improved.

Toward the end of our work together, she had another very powerful dream:

I was driving my car, consciously speeding to reach a group of friends. I heard the car screeching and suddenly realized I was out of control... the car careened through a busy parking lot and went over the side of a cliff. Then it paused in the air as I tried to get out of the seat belt.

Suddenly the car and I were back in the parking lot, safe and parked. A woman I know was at the passenger-side door looking at me intensely. I asked her what had happened, and she said that everyone watched the car go over, but it was as if the earth extended to hold me and I was able to drive back onto the lot. When she asked how I did it, I knew it was a miracle and said, "I only know that I feel very connected and cared for."

"When I awoke," she explained, "it was the first time I remember believing so strongly that a dream was real. And, dream or not, it felt like the perfect measure of what was becoming possible. As consciousness expands, the human vehicle is capable of much more; we see things differently and reality shifts accordingly."

What is revealed in our dreams through the light of consciousness provides profound insights into our inner life. According to early twentieth-century psychoanalyst Sigmund Freud, "The interpretation of dreams is the royal road to a knowledge of the unconscious activities of the mind." You might say that dreams distill consciousness, leading to new levels of understanding, enlightened action, and even greater clarity by day. The depth of vision experienced in our dreams provides us with a glimpse of our limitless nature. The question now is how to tap into this limitless nature in our waking life.

CHAPTER SIX

Escaping the Mind Field

A human being is a part of the whole, called by us the "Universe," a part limited in time and space. He experiences himself, his thoughts and feelings as something separated from the rest, a kind of optical delusion of his consciousness.... Our task must be to free ourselves from this prison by widening our circle of compassion to embrace all living creatures and the whole of nature in its beauty.

— ALBERT EINSTEIN

Who would we be if we forgot our name, age, gender, skin color, religion, preferences, state of health, and every other descriptor we use to differentiate ourselves from each other? What would our lives be like if we did not see each other as different from ourselves?

Many of the problems we encounter in our lives are due to the misperception that we are separate from one another, when we are actually inseparably connected to each other and everything else in the universe. We have all been conditioned by this limited view of reality to identify our mind and body as "me" and everything else as "not me," resulting in loneliness, envy, violence, and prejudice.

Every war, inquisition, ethnic cleansing, act of terror, and genocide is the external manifestation of our conditioned prejudice when someone's ideas, skin color, gender, religion, sexual nature, or physical appearance is different than our own. All these acts of violence are an attempt to extinguish the "not me" and assert the "me." Many wars have been carried out to prove that my God is better than yours.

But the real violence is the internal conflict we experience throughout our lives, because we do not know who we are and believe we are essentially different from others.

In his book *Wholeness and the Implicate Order*, renowned physicist David Bohm writes, "The widespread and pervasive distinctions between people...which are now preventing mankind from working together for the common good, and indeed, even for survival, have one of the key factors of their origin in a kind of thought that treats things as inherently divided."

If physicists proffer that the entire universe is comprised of a singular, luminous potential known as light (which we explored in the last chapter), and ancient mystical texts have historically referred to God and consciousness as light, then how does this illusion of separateness come into being?

The Mind Makes It Matter

At a fundamental level, all that exists is an ocean of infinite potentiality — endless possibilities that only manifest as specific outcomes when measured by a device or a person acting as an observer. In theory, the observer should not impact whatever is being observed, resulting in an objective observation. However, it has been scientifically demonstrated that this is impossible. We cannot detach ourselves from our experiences, as the observer and observed are inseparably linked in part by the observer's point of view.

Quantum physics gives us a glimpse of how the mind transforms a field of infinite possibilities into what appears to be distinct forms. The observer within us is the *conscious mind* whose point of view is a network of well-defined ideas, beliefs, and memories about what we have established as reality. According to its conditioned concepts, the conscious mind projects definition and meaning onto a formless environment, limiting its infinite possibilities into a subset that we call "reality." In this way, you can say that the mind transforms light (the formless) into matter and assigns meaning to that matter. As a result, the mind makes matter (any collection of atoms and molecules) matter (have significance).

As long as we continue to strictly view our experiences through the lens of the conscious mind, we remain locked in a circuit of duality. By judging our experiences as good or bad, right or wrong, black or white, we become enmeshed in our illusion of being separate from what we experience "out there." But as the Talmud, a central text of Rabbinic Judaism, states, "We do not see things as they are; we see them as we are" (Berakhot 55b). How we see ourselves is how we see the world. There is no experience without an experiencer. At the quantum level, nothing exists without an observer, for *there simply is no reality independent of consciousness.* So what is consciousness?

For many people consciousness is limited to *self*-consciousness, a state of being aware of oneself as well as one's internal and external environment. Consciousness extends far beyond this, however, and must be delineated into its *local* and *nonlocal* expressions.

Local consciousness is associated with the *conscious mind,* the everyday reality of form, ego, and choice created when a boundless universe is confined to a singular point of view. Nonlocal consciousness is associated with the *unconscious mind,* the formless, egoless, and choiceless infinite potential that exists before light is transformed into matter by the conscious mind's point of view. The unconscious is unavailable for analysis because there is no separate "self" to observe it. In *The Social Animal,* American journalist David Brooks writes, "If the conscious mind is like a general atop a platform who sees the world from a distance and analyzes things linearly and linguistically, the unconscious mind is like a million little scouts. The scouts career across the landscape, sending back a constant flow of signals and generating instant responses. They maintain no distance from the environment around them, but are immersed in it. They scurry about, interpenetrating other minds, landscapes and ideas."

We have all been conditioned to believe that we are in control of our lives. Yet most of what happens in life occurs outside our conscious awareness, and few things are within our control.

According to physicist Amit Goswami, author of *The Self-Aware Universe*, "The conscious self is unconscious of most things most of the time — and of everything in dreamless sleep. Paradoxically, the unconscious is…conscious of all things all of the time. It never sleeps."

Literally trillions of processes take place in our bodies every second, and we are totally unaware of them. None of us has to remind our heart to beat, our body to breathe, or the trillions of cells within us to replenish themselves. None of us awakens the sun, moves the tides, or changes the seasons. Yet most of us place such importance on who we think we are and the ideas traversing our awareness that we forget that most of our life runs without our control or thought.

Since the *conscious mind* of the ego and the *unconscious mind* of infinite potential are both aspects of our totality, why do we identify ourselves with the limited view of the conscious mind to the exclusion of the limitless view of the unconscious?

The Illusory Me

During early infancy, a child exists in a state that Sigmund Freud described as "oceanic bliss," unaware of anything other than its own boundlessness. This state of pure awareness exists because an infant's brain lacks the network of connections required to distinguish itself from the rest of the world. This innate lack of self-awareness demonstrates that we come into this world "hardwired" to experience oneness.

As a baby gradually develops and interacts with its environment and the individuals within it, they become increasingly aware of the response to their actions by those around them. While certain behaviors are met with acceptance, others are frowned upon and, at times, penalized. This initially confusing experience eventually trains the child to monitor and modify their own way of being in an attempt to "fit in" and behave in a way that is acceptable to those around them. "Self-talk" first emerges during this process of self-guidance and self-regulation of behavior.

Over time this comforting inner dialogue takes on a personality all its own, giving rise to an individual sense of *self* and to the corresponding neural circuitry required to sustain the illusion that the child is different from those around them. As a result, their natural and effortless way of being is gradually replaced by a series of *normal* conditioned behaviors. As the youngster matures and becomes increasingly more accustomed to the voice of the "illusory" ego, this commentary takes on a larger role in their life. They become habituated to interacting with it and eventually accept it as the real and authentic expression of their uniqueness.

The ego's roots, now well established, disguise the youth's boundless nature with this personality, whose self-importance convinces them that they are on their own and must *make things happen*. In an attempt to accomplish that, they habitually *think ahead*, hoping to control life by exerting their so-called free will.

Living in a Mind Field

This incessant pattern of worrying, planning, and rehearsing, which the Buddha referred to as *monkey mind*, becomes increasingly louder and more distracting as the individual tries to ensure that their actions are acceptable and their needs are met. The individual becomes so identified with the voice in their head that it transforms their mind into a hall of mirrors and their body into a living canvas of their thoughts.

Ultimately our intrinsic cooperative nature is displaced by a more competitive lifestyle aimed at producing safety, security, and predictability. But since there are no safety nets in a world that is constantly changing, our efforts often result in a great deal of stress and feelings of emptiness because our reality does not match up with our mental paradigm.

Based on the belief that we have free will, we assume there must be something wrong with us, or something we are doing or not doing that is interfering with our presumed ability to manifest the life we want. So we try to identify the problem, which is often blamed on one's *shadow*, and to learn *the secret* of how to attract what we want so we can live a happy and successful life.

We read book after book and attend workshop after workshop; we run in circles trying to chase away our shadow. But the faster we run, the faster our shadow follows us, never disappearing no matter what we do or where we go. If you saw someone chasing their shadow, you would think that person was crazy. And yet this is precisely what we do when we assume something is wrong with us. What we call our shadow is nothing more than an aspect of our nature waiting to be embraced and reclaimed. One of the consequences of seeing the world through the conscious mind is that we judge everything...and that includes us.

The idea that we are not enough the way we are is pernicious. Despite doing all the "right" things, such as meditating, eating right, and following a spiritual path — what we believe to be the recipe for enlightenment — real peace continues to elude us. I can truly relate to this formula, as I did many of these same things on my journey.

Many of us spend our lives trying to become the person we think we would have been were all our pieces left intact. After years of camouflaging my life with degrees that were earned in hopes of convincing the world I was smart, someone said to me, "You're constantly doing an impersonation of the person you already are." Like a dog who finally catches the tail they have been chasing only to realize it was their own, I finally recognized that *I already was the person I was trying to become.* To quote T. S. Eliot, "We shall not cease from exploration, and the end of all our exploring will be to arrive where we started and know the place for the first time."

The idea of self-improvement sounds wonderful. Yet it is often based on the idea that something is wrong with us and that we are separate from everything else. So we do everything we can in order to change, not realizing that we, as an integral part of the universe, are continually evolving. In the words of Greek philosopher Heraclitus, the only "constant is change."

We feel that the obstacles we face on our journey to wholeness are self-created and limit our growth, not realizing that the stress and sense of confinement that we feel are actually what fuels our development and evolution.

Consider how a lobster grows. A lobster is a spongy animal that lives in a rigid shell that does not expand. As the lobster grows its shell becomes uncomfortable and confining. To deal with this painful predicament, the lobster crawls under a rock where it feels safe from predatory fish, casts off its shell, and grows a new one. Throughout its life it repeats the process. Over and over again the lobster expands beyond its shell and goes into temporary safe seclusion until it develops a new shell that is secure and comfortable.

Everything in life grows in the same way. A stressor is required to spur the evolutionary process. So when you are uncomfortable it does not necessarily mean that you have done something wrong or are on the wrong track. It may just be the intelligence of life gently reminding you that it is time for change.

A shadow is produced when an object blocks light. Whenever we block the light guiding our life, we create a shadow. Only when we are transparent and in alignment with the source of the light, as when the sun is directly overhead, does the shadow magically disappear.

Our true awakening is the realization that nothing is wrong with us. We can only be who we already are in each moment. But this realization cannot be discovered while we look for it. It often comes when we least expect it.

In 2002, while sitting on my couch, my eyes just gazing at the walls, I became aware of the intricate molding at the edge of the ceiling, the beautiful artwork on the walls, and the clean, clear Zen-like quality present in my home. The beauty I noticed was a reflection of the way I saw and responded to everything in my life at that time.

Suddenly I felt as though honey was slowly being poured on the top of my head. I closed my eyes and noticed the sensation extending onto my forehead and temples. When it reached my eyes, tears began to flow down my face. I was overcome with the realization that there was nothing wrong with me — there had never been anything wrong with me. It was a moment of *unconditional acceptance*, a spontaneous gift of grace.

The Neurology of Transcendence

In 1973 I was introduced to the practice of meditation as a way to reduce stress and quiet the mind. After months of daily practice I was able to reach a deep state of quiescence — my troubles disappeared as physical sensation; mental chatter and emotional dissonance were minimized. Yet a silent, spacious awareness remained. These early experiences, along with the healing of my vision, which also occurred while meditating, were so profound that I wondered how the process of meditation altered our view of reality.

Using blood flow as an indicator of brain activity, Dr. Andrew Newberg, director of research at the Marcus Institute of Integrative Health, found that when Tibetan Buddhists were meditating they exhibited less activity in the brain area that creates a sense of separation between the self and the rest of existence, and more activity in the brain region that yields a sense of oneness. In addition, when Dr. Richard J. Davidson studied the Dalai Lama's most proficient meditators, Davidson, director of the Waisman Laboratory for Brain Imaging and Behavior, found a considerable increase in activity in the brain area associated with feelings of joy, happiness, and compassion, and extremely powerful gamma waves in that same area of the brain, indicating heightened consciousness and bliss. In further support of Newberg and Davidson's findings, Dr. Roeland Van Wijk found that biophoton emission in healthy transcendental meditation practitioners was 35 percent lower than the control group, indicating minimal light loss due to organismic integrity. Since consciousness is inseparable from our well-being and biophoton emission is lowest with optimum health, Van Wijk's research indicates that the body functions more harmoniously as we disconnect from our conditioned responses and come into a state of oneness with life.

Einstein said, "Beyond the tireless efforts of the investigator there lurks a stronger, more mysterious drive: it is existence and reality that one wishes to comprehend." Whether the drive to understand reality guides us to look through a microscope for the irreducible, through a telescope for the infinite, or through meditation for the seed of our existence, the goals of the scientist and the mystic are the same — to discover the source of who we are.

Merging into Oneness

We have grown so enamored with the conscious mind that we have forgotten that the only reason we are aware of its activity is because, in each instance, our undifferentiated essence is witnessing it. Unless we are experienced meditators, most of us bypass the purity of this witness. Instead, we listen to the familiar voice that emerges a millisecond later, commenting on that which has been witnessed. The voice of the conscious mind deliberates on whether something is good or bad, or whether we want it in our lives or not.

The witness and the conscious mind are like the sun and the moon — both appear to give off light. However, one is the source and the other its reflection. The witness is the sun, the limitless potential of the unconscious mind. The conscious mind, like the moon, reflects back a limited interpretation of reality through the lens of duality and conditioning. The conscious mind does not conceive; it merely considers a response to that which has been witnessed.

In the Gospel of Thomas, Jesus spoke about going beyond the duality of the conscious mind when he said, "When you make the two one...the inside like the outside and the outside like the inside...the above like the below...the male and the female one and the same...then will you enter the Kingdom."

We embrace the dichotomy of the conscious and unconscious minds, allowing both to merge with the unity of our nature, when we accept life as it is. Most of us experience only what we believe to be true or possible in our lives. But what if we were able to suspend our beliefs and simply witness and accept all that we see with no point of view? According to nineteenth-century poet William Blake, "If the doors of perception were cleansed everything would appear to man as it is, infinite."

When someone asks us who we are, we tell them our name. If they ask what we do, we tell them our occupation: a doctor, lawyer, plumber. When asked to describe ourselves, we say we are a man or woman, white or of color, married or single, gay or straight. But who are we without these labels?

We have all been trained to reduce the infinite possibilities of the universe into our own narrow prisonlike view. But do not be too concerned, as the confinement created by the ego is an integral part of our life's journey toward self-realization, eventually becoming the catalyst for our prison break and ultimate freedom.

In *The Essential Teachings of Ramana Maharshi*, the revered Indian sage states, "Thoughts arise because of the thinker. The thinker is the ego which, if sought, will automatically vanish." To penetrate the veil of the ego, Maharshi recommends that when thoughts arise, one should ask silently, "Who had this thought?" You will then probably hear, "me." Then ask, "Who am I?"

Each time I follow this suggestion, the illusion of *me*, as the chatter in my mind, infinitely expands, and all that remains is an all-inclusive spaciousness. The thinker of thoughts, performer of deeds, and sense of individuality disappear without a trace and what remains is pure awareness.

CHAPTER SEVEN

Discovering the Genius within Us

If the moon, in the act of completing its eternal way around the earth, were gifted with self-consciousness, it would feel thoroughly convinced that it was traveling its way of its own accord.... So would a Being, endowed with higher insight...watching man and his doings, smile about man's illusion that he was acting according to his own free will.

— ALBERT EINSTEIN

As human beings, we have been conditioned to believe that our thoughts are the sole cause of our actions. We have forgotten that inspiration — that which breathes and motivates us — is defined as "divine influence directly and immediately exerted upon the mind or soul." It is easy to forget the gift of this transmission when we constantly hear the expression, "We create our own reality." We forget that there would be no reality to "create" without the intuitive guidance that sparks our inspiration in the first place. This brings up an interesting question: How much *free will*, as an extension of the mind, do we actually have in response to this inspiration?

Although most of us find it comforting to believe that we are in control of our lives, neuroscientists have conducted studies revealing that only 5 percent of our cognitive activities — decisions, emotions, actions, behavior — are conscious, whereas the remaining 95 percent are generated by the unconscious. "Some researchers have gone so far as to suggest that the unconscious mind does virtually all the work and that conscious will may be an illusion," writes cognitive psychologist Timothy D. Wilson in *Strangers to Ourselves.*

The human brain has two very different processing systems. The first responds quickly, instinctually, and unconsciously. It is controlled by the right hemisphere and ancient limbic and "reptilian" parts of our brain. The second responds slowly, logically, and consciously, and it is controlled by the left hemisphere and the modern neocortex. Intuition is part of the first system, and researchers have found that it provides us immediate answers that are usually correct, long before the second system even gets started. Some of these studies have even demonstrated that our physiology, or our bodily functions, can predict the correct answer two to three seconds before a computer-generated question has even been posed.

During a conversation with Shinichi Suzuki, the great pioneer of musical education, Albert Einstein said, "The theory of relativity occurred to me by intuition, and music is the driving force behind this intuition. My parents had me study the violin from the time I was six. My new discovery is the result of musical perception."

Since modern technology can now study the brain in real time, scientists are watching the decision-making process at work and arriving at some startling conclusions.

In 2007 Dr. John-Dylan Haynes, a neuroscientist at the Bernstein Center for Computational Neuroscience in Berlin, conducted a series of experiments using a functional MRI. Placing subjects in a brain scanner with a display screen that flashed a succession of random letters, he instructed participants to press a button with either their right or left index finger whenever they felt the urge — and to remember the letter they saw on the screen the moment they decided which finger to use. Haynes and his team were able to determine their subjects' decisions about which finger to use up to seven seconds before the subjects were aware of making them.

Haynes and his team then asked the participants to decide whether to add or subtract two numbers from a numeric series presented on a screen. When presented with more complex problems, the subjects displayed decision-making brain activity four seconds before they themselves were conscious of making those decisions.

A four- to seven-second advanced response on the part of the brain may seem like a relatively short period of time, but when we consider that twenty quadrillion bits of information move around our brain every second, a few seconds is highly significant.

The individuals in these studies were sure that their decisions were the result of conscious deliberation — their own free will — which makes one wonder: How can we be sure that we made a choice, if we do not actually know how or when that choice was made?

Although these carefully controlled and replicated studies cannot totally rule out the existence of free will, they do indicate that our actions are not so much influenced by conscious choices as by something within us that knows what we are going to do even before we consciously decide to do it. The something within us, often referred to as our intuition, inner knowing, or "higher self," knows what is best for us even if we do not understand why.

Although we have been led to believe that we are continually making conscious choices, Haynes's research clearly demonstrates that our precognitive capacities are far greater than previously imagined.

Follow Your Heart

Further confirming Haynes's research, Dr. Rollin McCraty at the Institute of HeartMath found that the heart has a precognitive sense of future events in the same way the brain does. McCraty and his team flashed a series of randomly selected pictures with either neutral or heightened emotional content to a group of subjects while monitoring their physiology. At the conclusion of the experiment, researchers had a record of which pictures each subject was shown, in what order they saw them, and how their physiology responded to each image viewed.

After processing the data, they found that each participant's physiology responded in a way that correlated with the emotional content of each image. Their physiology was agitated when they viewed an emotionally charged picture and tranquil when they viewed an emotionally neutral one. This was normal and to be expected.

What was unexpected, however, was that their hearts not only responded seconds before their brains did but also before each picture flashed on the screen. Up to six seconds before a subject saw a frightening image, their hearts already revealed an arousal response and informed their brains accordingly, giving new meaning to the expression that we know something "by heart." But it is more than our heart; it is also our instinctive sense of knowing, or gut feeling, about the things we encounter in the world.

These studies clearly demonstrate that we have an internal GPS that navigates what we consider to be *our* choices or responses, precognitively. This is not unreasonable when we recall the quantum principle that the conscious (or local) mind *thinks* it knows, while the unconscious (or nonlocal) mind *knows* without knowing that it knows! What, then, is the role of conscious thought, which we have all been conditioned to lead with?

In a paper recently published in the journal *Behavioral and Brain Sciences*, a group of researchers led by associate professor of neuroscience Ezequiel Morsella of San Francisco State University concluded that nearly all the brain's work is conducted at the unconscious level. When that processing is complete and there is a physical act to perform, that very small job is implemented by the conscious mind.

In essence, we barely control our thinking process even though the conscious mind appears busy at work and is happy to take all the credit. Even when we are speaking, the content of our speech is first composed for us by the unconscious mind.

In 1977 I was asked to give a presentation to a group of graduate students at Florida International University. I spent hours preparing my speech and made notes on forty index cards. As I walked from the wings to the podium I realized that I had written and rehearsed every sentence of a lecture about a subject on which I was supposedly "an expert." Suddenly the index cards I prepared so meticulously slipped out of my hands and scattered on the stage floor. It all happened so fast that I had no time to pick them up — so I just kept walking, stepped behind the dais, and tried to collect myself.

After what felt like an eternity, I took a deep breath and shared with the audience what happened. At first, several people laughed. Then the entire group and I sighed in unison as if the weight of the world had been lifted from our shoulders. There was now no need for either of us to perform. My one-hour presentation on learning disabilities turned into a three-hour informal discussion about *learning without effort*. I walked away that day knowing that I never again had to prepare a lecture, or anything for that matter, in advance — so long as I knew it by heart and trusted what flowed through me effortlessly.

After presenting more than two thousand lectures, seminars, and workshops in this same manner, I have come to realize that the message that is shared does not necessarily originate from the thinking mind. As vehicles of life's intelligence, we are designed to express our unique gifts and purpose for being in a seamless fashion. Let me illustrate what I mean.

One day a patient came in complaining of blurry vision. I asked her to read the eye chart and the smallest line she could see was 20/80, which confirmed her symptoms. For some reason, however, my eyes felt drawn to an area on the left side of her upper back, behind her heart. I was not sure why. With the eye chart still projected, I asked if she would feel comfortable if I placed a hand lightly on her back. As soon as I did, she said "Wow" and proceeded to read the entire eye chart with *100 percent accuracy*. I do not know what occurred physiologically, but I do know that something guided me to that spot.

The more I tried to figure out how such phenomena occur, the less I understood. Yet within this paradox lived a truth that would impact all my work going forward: whenever I focused on *one thing*, I missed everything *I was not looking for*. In trying to figure things out to help the patient, my field of vision contracted, confining my view to the solution I thought I was after. An infinite field of possibilities dramatically narrowed as my conscious mind tried to figure out something that my intuition already knew. When I opened my focus, however, my awareness expanded and I became conscious of what was catching my eye. In other words, any attempt to make things happen versus noticing what was calling me limited my perception. The more comfortable I grew looking for nothing, the more profound my experiences with patients became. However, I was no longer satisfied just doing eye exams and being an optometrist. I wanted to understand what it truly means *to see*.

To understand what it means to see, however, we must look deeper than the mechanisms of the physical eye to truly comprehend the source of our seeing. Who — or what — is behind the *eye* of our vision, the *ear* of our hearing, the *mouth* of our speaking, and the *breath* of our inspiration?

If we are fortunate enough to perceive the source behind these mysteries, we might also discover that we are not so much living life as *life is living us*. And although what we experience is constantly changing, "we" remain the same. According to thirteenth-century Sufi poet Jalal ad-Din Rumi, "Everything you see has its roots in the unseen world. The forms may change, yet the essence remains the same. Every wonderful sight will vanish; every sweet word will fade, but do not be disheartened, the source they come from is eternal, growing, branching out, giving new life and new joy."

Creation Is Collaborative

If creation is the transformation of the unseen to seen, formless to form, concept to construct — and nonlocal consciousness is the field of infinite possibilities associated with the unconscious mind — it would seem that the unconscious mind is the most probable source from which inspiration arises. When the conscious mind is illuminated with inspiration via the unconscious mind, it is then galvanized into a state of *excitation*, followed by *implementation*, all of which leads to *manifestation*.

The implementation phase may require consideration, which is where conscious thought becomes an integral part of the creative process. Once the unconscious directs and the conscious implements, the dance of collaborative creation begins. When we busy ourselves trying to *make things happen* without inspiration, however, we are left with feelings of solitude and desperation, a kind of self-generated anxiety that occupies our mind much of the time. According to a Japanese proverb, "Vision without action is a daydream. Action without vision is a nightmare."

We are so accustomed to trying to make things happen in our lives that we assume that we alone are responsible for our life experiences. However, we must remember that nothing occurs by itself. Everything in life is interconnected. We do not even breathe on our own. Life is continuously breathing us and inspiring us. Life is a creative and collaborative process — a true partnership.

Awakening is not a question of *thy will be done* versus *my will be done*. It is not about remaining choiceless or making choices but rather recognizing that just as it takes two to tango, the unconscious and conscious minds exist in order to join forces in the creative process.

Henry David Thoreau writes, "The eye revolves upon an independent pivot which we can no more control than our own will. Its axle is the axle of the soul, as the axis of the earth is coincident with the axis of the heavens." In other words, we are inseparably connected to the intelligence of life, whose directives inspire and animate our actions.

Maybe it is time to put our index cards and PowerPoint presentations aside and begin living life by heart. Our mental rehearsals attempt to ensure that things go *our way*, but we will never develop the ability to traverse the tightrope of life until we are able to do it without a net. The depth of our genius only reveals itself when we embrace each moment without conscious safeguards, trusting the guidance that comes to us freely.

Discovering the Genius Within

According to Einstein, "All great achievements of science must start from intuitive knowledge. I believe in intuition and inspiration.... At times I feel certain I am right while not knowing the reason." Thus, his famous statement that for creative work in science, "imagination is more important than knowledge."

Many important discoveries and insights occur when we are not looking for them, such as Alexander Fleming's accidental discovery of penicillin. Safety glass, smoke detectors, and x-ray imaging, along with many of today's most popular medications, were inadvertently stumbled upon. In addition, a study of European inventors, published in 2005, discovered that 50 percent of patents were the result of ideas that emerged when inventors were working on unrelated projects or when they were not trying to invent anything.

We often ascribe serendipitous or synchronous events to luck. But analytical psychologist Carl Jung, who first introduced this theory in the 1920s, believed that events can be logically connected by cause and effect, or they can be linked in ways that are evidently meaningful, even though the reason for their connection is not obvious or easy to explain. Jung designated incidents that are apparently related even though they share no causal relationship as "meaningful coincidences."

Today physicists explain synchronicity as an example of quantum entanglement, where two or more particles (or two or more ideas, people, or events) that were once linked remain infinitely connected regardless of distance, so when one particle is affected by an action, analogous changes are observed in the others.

The word *serendipity*, which means "pleasant surprise," originated from a Persian fairy tale about three princes from the Isle of Serendip who possessed superpowers of observation. But serendipity is not merely a random stroke of good fortune. It describes how our *inner genius* guides us.

The word *genius* was originally defined as the "guiding spirit" of a person or place. Our greatest joy is often the result of the unexpected surprises and magical moments that occur when we "absentmindedly" follow that guiding spirit and experience the miracles that manifest as a result. The true story below, shared by a close friend, beautifully illustrates this point.

Bill Thompson was feeling overworked and in need of a break. Owning and running a popular hardware store in Ohio was his life, and it was time for a deep breath. He went out with a good friend to a local bar, had a few drinks, and talked about feeling too much pressure and not having enough time to fish. A few seats down from him at the bar, a man authoritatively and without permission offered this opinion. "I know of the best fishing excursion you'll ever have in your life. It's in Alaska. Have you been to Alaska? Well, if you haven't, you need to go. I know a man who will take you out on his boat, provide you with all the fishing and camping gear that you'll need, and drop you off on your own private little island, totally uninhabited, where you can fish for days and clear your soul, all alone. I promise you, your life will change forever."

Bill was not impressed with his self-appointed vacation advisor but somehow knew he would make the trip. He felt he had to for whatever reason.

A month later he was flying to Alaska. He had never done anything like a solo wilderness fishing trip. He was excited, intrigued, and afraid of being alone. After a second plane ride — a rough flight on a small and seemingly ancient backcountry aircraft — he reached the small seaside village where the outfitter ran his business for adventure fishing. Bill agreed to do a three-day solo trip. His guide provided him with some unimpressive camping equipment, along with food and all the fishing gear he would need. It was a two-hour boat ride to his island through the cold Alaskan waters.

Bill's experience was quiet and thoughtful; warm by day and cool at night. The ocean was plentiful. He ate the best fish he had ever caught, dreamed each night of his childhood, and wished for more love in his life. After three days he felt renewed. His guide returned as promised with another vacationing fisherman who was on the boat. The guide had dropped him off a day earlier on another island. They would make the journey back to the village together.

As Bill started loading his gear onto the boat, the other fisherman screamed out in delight, "Jesse, I can't believe what I'm seeing! It's you! Why didn't you tell me you were coming here? I can't believe it!" Bill was uncomfortable with this case of mistaken identity. How could someone be so wrong in identifying what seemed like a friend he knew so well? "I'm sorry. You've got me mixed up with someone else," he said.

The man continued to insist that Bill was Jesse until he finally realized that Bill was quite serious and he was not his friend. "Well then, you've absolutely got to have a twin brother," the man said defiantly.

For a moment time stopped, and Bill felt the tears streaming down his face. "I do have a twin brother," he said. "We were separated when we were four years old. Our mom gave us up for adoption. My brother's name is Jesse. That's all I know. I haven't seen him in thirty-six years." Without another thought, the two men embraced each other and both began to cry.

On the boat ride back to the village the fisherman explained that Jesse was one of his best friends. They lived in Northern California. Jesse was a carpenter. The two were surely identical twins. And yes, Jesse had mentioned his brother a while back, whom he longed for and dreamed about for so many years.

The twins reunited weeks later in California. The man in the bar was right. It was a fishing trip that would change his life forever.

Our resistance to the flow of life is like swimming upstream — it takes effort. The same is true of using our will to get our way. The more energy we exert, the more resistance we experience. And if we do not get our way, it only reinforces the illusion that no matter what we do, we cannot get it right.

But when we realize that the navigational system within us is inseparable from that which animates everything in the universe, our illusion of individuality dissolves. We grow lighter and start seeing life with new eyes.

As my parents approached their deaths, I asked them if they had found anything in life they could actually control.

My mother said, "It's not in our hands."

My father said, "You just have to be with things as they are."

Those statements, coming from two people who had lived more than ninety years each, gave me great appreciation for the Yiddish proverb they often said: *Der mentsh trakht un Got lakht*, "Man plans and God laughs."

In his book *Anam Cara: A Book of Celtic Wisdom*, the poet John O'Donohue writes, "Your soul knows the geography of your destiny. Your soul alone has the map of your future, therefore you can trust this indirect, oblique side of yourself. If you do, it will take you where you need to go, but more important it will teach you a kindness of rhythm in your journey." The kindness of rhythm that you learn on life's journey is but one of the gifts you will receive by following your inner guidance. But perhaps the most essential gift is lasting contentment.

CHAPTER EIGHT

Awareness Is Curative

Awareness is the greatest alchemy there is.

— OSHO

A middle-aged woman came to see me because she was born cross-eyed. She had had three surgeries to correct it, and as a result her eyes were aligned, but she saw double all the time. She could not read or drive, and she had to wear a patch on one eye. She said the quality of her life was awful.

After hearing her story, I had a sudden "flash of insight" and realized that I might be able to help her. Without telling her exactly what I was doing, I removed her patch and placed a soft contact lens on each eye, so that one eye could see clearly at distance and the other could see clearly up close.

I checked her visual acuity with both eyes open and found that she could easily read 20/20 at both far and near. I then asked her to stand up, walk around the office, step outside for a few minutes, and then tell me how she felt. When she returned, she said that the contact lenses felt comfortable and that she could see very clearly. Suddenly she exclaimed, "Oh my God, I'm not seeing double!" I smiled with the satisfaction of knowing that I might be able to help her.

After a moment she turned to me with a strange look on her face and said, "I don't think you understand my problem." She then started to tell me her history again, although I had already heard it. I explained to her what I had done and why she was no longer seeing double, but the woman was unable to embrace the possibility of living without the problem she had endured her entire life.

This experience reminded me of a story of a man who went to his doctor, spent a great deal of time telling him about his chronic back pain, and then asked the doctor if he could help him. The doctor examined the man's back, took x-rays, and then told him what he could do to alleviate his pain. The man immediately said that he did not think that approach would work. The doctor listened and then asked the man to at least try it for a week to see if it helped. But the man kept insisting that he did not think it would work. Finally, the doctor said, "I think I can alleviate your back pain, but there is a risk that you'll be left with nothing to talk about."

Difficult life experiences can often fix our point of view, making it hard for us to consider the possibility that our lives could be different. However, as circumstances change, our point of view can gradually soften and our field of perception may expand, allowing us to *see* that our so-called problems may be part of the solution — and ultimately our road to liberation. If we are fortunate enough to experience life with no point of view, even for a short period of time, consciousness expands, catalyzing profound change that is sometimes instantaneous.

In her *New York Times* bestseller *Radical Remission: Surviving Cancer against All Odds*, Dr. Kelly A. Turner found that almost every radical remission cancer survivor she studied indicated that they used their intuition to guide decisions related to their healing process. According to Dr. Turner, the survivors she studied learned how to use the guidance provided by the parts of the brain that developed at a time in human evolution when danger was an integral part of everyday survival.

Since most of us today live in relatively safe environments, the limbic and reptilian parts of our brain, which quickly and accurately sense danger and know how to avoid it, are often not used. But these brain structures are not just valuable for detecting and avoiding danger. These intricate levels of inner knowing, which include the intuitive centers of the brain, also allow us to develop an authentic trust in life and the guidance it provides us.

Since intuition emerges from the infinite potential of the unconscious, its guidance leads to a unique level of spacious awareness that often has medicinal value. This may be the reason why intuition played such a significant role in the healing process of Dr. Turner's subjects.

Guidance that emerges from our unconscious provides a level of pure awareness that has the potential to be profoundly curative, because it comes from the same source that activates and regulates the entire universe. Revered Indian guru Nisargadatta Maharaj spoke of the power of awareness when he said, "As the sun on rising makes the world active, so does self-awareness affect changes in the mind. In the light of calm and steady self-awareness, inner energies wake up and work miracles without any effort on your part."

The relationship between the mind and body has been investigated since the beginning of modern medicine. But it was not until 1985 that research conducted by neuropharmacologist Dr. Candace Pert revealed that there are mechanisms through which the emotions, originating in our limbic system, affect our immune system, creating a deeply interdependent feedback loop.

Dr. Pert's discoveries, along with those of other mind-body pioneers, demonstrate that our every thought, idea, and belief materializes into a chemical messenger that impacts our physiology and is simultaneously experienced by every cell of the body. These findings indicate that every state of mind manifests as molecules known as neuropeptides, neurotransmitters, hormones, and pheromones. This discovery has become the foundation of mind-body medicine or psychoneuroimmunology.

How we perceive life determines how our experiences impact us emotionally and physiologically. The mental and emotional meanings we associate with certain experiences result in a cascade of different messenger molecules, directing our cells to speed up, slow down, migrate, reproduce, and even die. Our *beliefs* about life have even more impact on our health and happiness than the actual experiences themselves.

Most disease is caused by stress, and most stress is the result of a mismatch between our beliefs about life and our actual life experiences. We place a great deal of importance on our beliefs because we are sure they are true. Yet when we consult a thesaurus we discover that although *belief* is synonymous with *thinking* and *idea*, it means the opposite of *truth*. If our beliefs direct our physiology, then perhaps many of our physical and emotional ailments are the result of our bodies being misdirected by ideas that are in conflict with our well-being.

The discovery of how our beliefs and emotions impact our physiology has given rise to many therapeutic approaches focused on changing beliefs and resolving emotional issues. But what happens if we no longer view life through the beliefs and ideas that form our point of view and instead accept life as it unfolds in each moment?

After working with thousands of individuals, I have come to see that the more we embrace what life brings us, the greater our contentment. And the more we reject it, the greater our stress and imbalance. So how can we begin to see life through no point of view and what will the effect of it be?

Open Focus

While experimenting with how different states of consciousness affected my vision, I was guided to practice seeing from a place *behind my head*. I imagined that the mechanism that was seeing within me was located about twelve to eighteen inches behind and slightly above my head. To my surprise, when I made this switch I experienced a radical shift. It felt as though I was in an altered state, looking at nothing in particular from a place with a limitless view. Suddenly my visual field expanded, resulting in a wide-angled and more telescopic perspective. This resulted in a deep trust in my ability to *see without looking*. The more I practiced this technique while walking and driving, the easier it was for me to access this perspective. I also noticed that if I had any physical pain or discomfort, it seemed to disappear as long as I remained in this state.

I began practicing this technique whenever I had a headache or other physical pain. If I imagined seeing from a place slightly above and behind my head, sure enough, the pain disappeared. After a while I began to realize that most of our physical discomfort is not caused by physical pain but rather by our habitual identification with the mind's beliefs about pain and the suffering that often accompanies it.

By seeing from a place with no point of view, the mental glue that keeps our pain intact often dissolves. Having guided my elderly mother, my children, and many of my clients through this process, I found it to be effective in alleviating headaches and dental pain, just to name a few causes of suffering. Seeing in this new way became natural for me, and I realized that it felt similar to the state of *pure awareness* I entered when my eyesight instantly cleared in 1976. But what is awareness, and can it be "curative" in dealing with other physical ailments?

What Is Awareness?

When we speak about awareness, most of us imagine focusing our attention on something in particular. It implies that there is a subject (who is conscious) and an object (that one is conscious of). This definition suggests that we view the world through the lens of the conscious mind. Although we often equate the term *awareness* with the activity of the mind, it is actually something entirely different. The conscious mind, or ego, lives by discernment and can never transcend duality. Duality itself is strictly a mental construct that infers an observer and an observed. Pure awareness, however, is synonymous with nonduality and only exists when the mind is transcended. It is, in essence, a state of no-mind.

As we become more conscious, we witness more of what is occurring inside and outside of us — our thoughts, feelings, and actions. And as we witness more, the mental "I" gradually disappears, leaving only pure awareness. Expanded levels of consciousness awaken the witness, whose subjectivity eventually dissolves, leaving only awareness — a field of eyes that sees without looking, or pure *isness*.

Expanded consciousness, such as the intuition that Dr. Turner's cancer survivors used to guide their healing process, is an integral aspect of medicine, as clinical practice has always been both an art and a science. While today's electronic health-care record systems frequently offer evidence-based decision-making support, a doctor must follow the most important clinical tool, their intuition. Here is an example of how accurately our intuition can function, even at long distances.

Years ago, my mother told me that her gynecologist detected something suspicious during an exam and recommended she have a hysterectomy. I wanted to know what the doctor found. My mother said the doctor was unsure but felt it would be a good idea to have a hysterectomy anyway, as my mother had already had repeated bouts with cancer.

At that moment, even though I was two thousand miles away, I "saw" my mother clearly and could see that she had a mass on her left side below the waist, but I knew that she did not need surgery. I told her that what she had was not cancer and suggested that she get a second opinion. So she went to another doctor who said that, based on the first doctor's report, they would also recommend a hysterectomy. I told my mother once again that I was sure she did not have cancer and did not need any surgery.

"How do you know?" she asked.

"Because I can see it."

By this time my parents were getting upset with me because they were used to following doctors' orders, even though I had helped my mother recover from blindness years earlier, when other doctors told her nothing could be done for her.

I do not know exactly how many gynecologists and surgeons my mother saw, but they all suggested that she have a hysterectomy based on the first doctor's report. I asked my mother to go to just one more specialist and have him call me while she was in the office. I agreed to go along with his recommendation, if she was willing to let me speak with him.

The following week she went to see a new doctor and called me during his evaluation. When I asked what he recommended, he too suggested a hysterectomy based on my mother's history with cancer.

I asked, "If this was your mother, what diagnostic tests would you recommend to be sure she needed the surgery?"

"Well, for sure an MRI."

"Has she had an MRI?"

After a long pause, he said, "No, but I'll order it."

My mother's MRI showed that she had a benign fibroid tumor and did not need surgery.

Trusting our inner guidance can profoundly impact not only our own lives but also the lives of those around us. It has the power to unlock a deeper level of seeing, allowing us to navigate our daily experiences with grace and without any forethought.

Seeing Without the Eyes

We are all so used to looking with our eyes that we have forgotten what it is like to see without them. This is one of the greatest benefits of trusting our inner vision and its guidance. It allows us to *see* without placing any stress on our eyes. When we trust in this nonphysical aspect of our vision, our physical eyes relax and remain flexible, efficient, and resilient. Since relying more deeply on this "inner" vision, I have found that I, at age seventy, can see with ease both near and far without the use of glasses.

Here is what my optometrist had to say:

> For the entire time Dr. Liberman has been a patient, he has not needed or depended on glasses to see. This was initially surprising to me since I first saw him at age sixty, and his prescription revealed moderate amounts of astigmatism. I also expected that he would need reading glasses. However, he was able to read 20/20 at near without any correction. Now, at age seventy, even though he exhibits more farsightedness and astigmatism than before, he is still able to read and see clearly without the aid of spectacles. In my thirteen years of experience practicing as an optometrist, I have not seen a person of Jacob's age and prescription seeing as well as he does without glasses.

Seeing through the Eyes of God

These experiences have reminded me that our true essence is *pure awareness*, a field of nonphysical vision that *witnesses* what we call life. Unfortunately, we have been led to believe that we only see with the physical eyes. But what if we are all actually *seeing through the eyes of God?* According to medieval Christian mystic Meister Eckhart, "The eye through which I see God is the same eye through which God sees me; my eye and God's eye are one eye, one seeing, one knowing, one love."

Ninth-century Buddhist master Lin Chi said, "If you meet the Buddha on the road, kill him," because if you see the Buddha outside of yourself, then it is not him. God, Buddha, Source, and Witness all reside within. Ramana Maharshi refers to *pure awareness* as the Self, and the Self as God. In his book *Power, Freedom, and Grace: Living from the Source of Lasting Happiness*, Deepak Chopra shares the Vedic expression, "I am not in the world; the world is in me. I am not in the body; the body is in me. I am not in the mind; the mind is in me. The body, mind, and world are my creation as I curve back within myself and create again and again." With the realization that we are pure awareness, our incessant desire to push life subsides, and acceptance and ease emerge.

In Taoism, they refer to this state as *wei wu wei*, or action without action. Others call it *nondoing*. It is not about hanging out and not accomplishing anything. This state of awareness employs a fluid response to life's guidance. Competitive athletes refer to nondoing as "being in the zone." In this state, an appropriate response to any situation occurs naturally, unedited by the intellect. It occurs with the recognition that the animating force of life always has the first move. Thus, our actions are not isolated initiations based on the conscious mind's desires but rather are responses to life's invitations. Nondoing indicates that we automatically respond to whatever life brings us; we feel no need to initiate anything. Lao Tzu expressed this beautifully when he said, "By letting it go it all gets done.... But when you try and try the world is beyond the winning."

When we imagine the animating force of the universe — the foundation of everything that is — most people envision something outside of themselves that is all-seeing, all-knowing, and omnipresent. By definition, such a force would have to be aware of and inseparable from everything we think, say, and do to effectively guide us. If we look carefully, we might discover that such a force, however we choose to name it, is always present and aware within us. Everything is constantly changing, except that which is witnessing. *We* are the indivisible field of awareness that is always present and independent of the physical, mental, and emotional experiences of the mind-body. Everything comes and goes except *awareness*.

Just as we have been conditioned to believe that "we" are the illusory *ego* assembled within the mind and brain, this conditioning can also be disassembled because *awareness is curative*. The curative power of awareness, or *being* as Plato called it, was noted in Plato's dialogue *The Sophist*, written in 360 BCE: "My notion would be that anything which possesses any sort of power to affect another, or to be affected by another, if only for a single moment, however trifling the cause and however slight the effect, has real existence; and I hold that the definition of being is simply power."

Our identification with the conscious mind is what feeds the illusion that allows the ego to grow beyond its purpose. However, as we identify more and more with the *witness* instead of the mind chatter, we witness more. Our consciousness expands, unleashing unexpected potential that permeates our waking life. In Zen Buddhism the portal to this expanded state is called a *satori* (or a "kick in the third eye"), and it is said to signal an illumination of one's truest nature. According to Lao Tzu, "He who knows others is wise. He who knows himself is enlightened."

Although seeing in our normal waking state is limited by our beliefs, under certain conditions our vision has the potential to surpass these restrictions, unearthing our natural state of pure awareness. One of the phenomena that has been rigorously investigated by science are the reports by individuals who have had near-death experiences and were considered by professionals to be medically dead.

In a thirteen-year study on near-death experiences published in the prestigious journal *Lancet*, researchers found that 12 percent of cardiac arrest survivors reported a near-death experience. Twenty-four percent of those patients accurately recalled events that occurred during their cardiac arrest, when there was no electrical activity in their brain. After reviewing and summarizing substantiation from an array of peer-reviewed studies on near-death experiences, University of Virginia School of Medicine researcher Edward Kelly and his colleagues stated the following in their book *Irreducible Mind*: "Such evidence, we believe, fundamentally conflicts with the conventional doctrine that brain processes produce consciousness, and supports the alternative view that brain activity normally serves as a kind of filter, which somehow constrains the material that emerges into waking consciousness."

But do we have to have a near-death experience to awaken? Why not have a near-life experience and get the same results? Perhaps our own direct experience is the key to awakening an entirely new way of seeing.

CHAPTER NINE

What Takes Your Breath Away

Breath is the bridge which connects life to consciousness, which unites your body to your thoughts. Whenever your mind becomes scattered, use your breath as the means to take hold of your mind again.

— THICH NHAT HANH

Throughout history, human beings have employed prayer, meditation, yoga, diet, martial arts, psychotropic drugs, and guru devotion in hopes of awakening. Having used several of these practices during my life's journey, I can attest to their value. Eventually, however, I realized that awakening, for me, was not about employing specific disciplines meant to quiet the mind, cleanse the body, or experience an altered state of consciousness. It was about gradually undressing my ego to reveal my natural state of being.

To accomplish that, I spent a great deal of time noticing what was naturally *catching my eye* and what was normally obstructing my view of the world around me. As I became aware of the ongoing conversation occurring in my mind, I also noticed that I was holding my breath, inadvertently suffocating my cells. This revelation helped me recognize that our breath is much more than just our breath.

More than six thousand years ago Chinese sages observed that life perpetually brings itself into balance through a process of alternating states of expansion and contraction. Nature has a universal order: a rise in anything is followed by its fall, an increase by decrease, and any exacerbation by remission. This primal rhythm, referred to as *yin* and *yang*, can be observed in all aspects of nature, and moving with its flow brings us into harmony with the animating force of life.

In the body this *primordial pulse* is evident in every physiological function from our breath and heartbeat to our craniosacral rhythm and vision. The body is always seeking homeostasis. We tend to think of this recurring rhythm as the respiratory cycle and believe that "we" are initiating this process. But our breathing cycle is intimately interwoven with the breathing cycle of every other living thing, including the earth, the solar system, and the universe itself. That which is breathing life into the infinite universe is also breathing life into us. This fundamental flow is the *heartbeat of life* — the *frequency of wellness*.

Hazrat Inayat Khan, founder of the Sufi Order in the West, said, "In the heart of man the whole universe is reflected; and as the whole universe is reflected in it, man may be called the heart of the universe." This expression of interconnectedness exists because the heart and the universe share the same shape and produce a similar electromagnetic field. In addition, the heart, the breath, and the universe share the same spiral movement pattern.

When this homeodynamic process is flowing freely, our heart and our breath are coordinating harmoniously, and we are in a state of physiological coherence, responding to life effortlessly with presence, clarity, and grace. Our physical health and emotional wellness significantly improve, and our eyes appear illuminated as an expression of *radiant* health. Abiding in this state also heightens intuition, providing us guidance and information about events that have not yet occurred.

Any effort or tension, however, restricts the breath, tightens the muscles, narrows awareness, dims the eye light, and lowers performance because the heart of the cosmos is motion, and anything that interferes with its movement obstructs life, health, and wellness. To experience our full potential we must reestablish this natural state of "flow" by recognizing that our breath is the most fundamental expression of this primal rhythm and a constant reflection of our connection with the source of all life. The word *spirit*, from the Latin *spiritus*, means "breath" and is also associated with "light." Anything that interrupts the breath weakens the life force, diminishing our light. When we hold our breath, we obstruct our ability to see, be, and respond to life.

According to pioneering psychotherapist and author Alexander Lowen, "Spirit is not a mystical concept. The spirit of a person is manifested in his aliveness, in the brightness of his eyes, in the resonance of his voice and in the ease and gracefulness of his movements." Our spirit, our breath, and our light are inseparable.

In *The Book Thief*, Markus Zusak writes, "How do you tell if something's alive? You check for breathing." Breathing is a reflection of our degree of aliveness. Those who breathe naturally with ease rarely get sick and tend to live a lot longer. Yet most people hold their breath or breathe in a shallow, irregular manner. That may be one reason why smoking cigarettes was so popular for so many years. It may have been the only time that a person actually breathed deeply. The fluidity of our breath is a reflection of the fluidity of our life. So why do we hold our breath so much? What takes our breath away, and what brings it back?

I Think, Therefore I Am

From early on we have been taught that we are the most evolved creatures on the planet. We are encouraged to use our mind to conceive new ideas, make appropriate choices, and solve problems. After years of being told to think ahead and that a mind is *a terrible thing to waste*, we have become addicted to thinking. According to the Laboratory of Neuro Imaging, the average human has about seventy thousand thoughts per day. This occurs in the privacy of our mind, under the guise that we are involved in an intellectual process. But is most of our thinking creative in nature, or is it primarily worrying about the unknown, mentally changing the subject whenever we feel uncomfortable, or rehearsing in hopes that things turn out our way?

Having had a reading problem as a child, I spent a great deal of time worrying about schoolwork and trying to figure out what I had to do in order to pass. Sometimes it involved cheating — looking at another person's test paper because I was sure they had the right answers. But then I realized that real cheating is not what occurs externally but internally — the *internal planning* we hide from others and from ourselves. And yet *we* see it. We are aware of it but do not realize that we are actually cheating ourselves of the opportunity to discover our true genius.

When we think, worry, or try to figure something out, we automatically hold our breath, and the answer we are looking for gets stuck on the tip of our tongue. Yet when we stop thinking and trying, the answer comes to us effortlessly in a flash of insight. As Albert Einstein said, "The intellect has little to do on the road to discovery. There comes a leap in consciousness, call it intuition or what you will, and the solution comes to you and you do not know how or why." Each time we hold a thought, we hold our breath. Rather than "I think, therefore I am," perhaps "I breathe, therefore I receive."

Make Your Life Your Meditation

Most people only notice the tendency to hold their breath when they are feeling anxious. I realized this in 1978, when I was in the midst of a breakdown. I was having panic attacks and noticed how difficult it was to breath. With so many emotional highs and lows, I needed to find a way to stay centered. Since breath awareness is the doorway into a meditative state, my meditation practice became a major source of stability.

Although I was meditating for twenty minutes once or twice a day, it was only a drop in the bucket when compared to the other sixteen hours I was awake. Everything was calmer while I was meditating, but shortly thereafter I often found myself back on an emotional roller coaster, unable to maintain the same level of peace inside myself. So I tried something different that, to my amazement, was easy and reduced my anxiety as well as the number of panic attacks I was experiencing. But before I reveal my discovery and explain how to do it, let me first share why I feel this is so beneficial.

The work of Dr. Andrew Newberg demonstrates that our brain is wired to experience two distinctly different realities. In everyday reality, we see the external world through the eyes of duality and the limited beliefs of the ego. During meditation, however, input from the external world is significantly diminished, and life is experienced through the eye of nonduality and oneness.

Our awakening depends on a shift in perception from identifying our self as the chattering mind to realizing that we are actually *pure awareness* — the awareness that witnesses the continual changes occurring in the mind and body. As this shift occurs, our brain function is redirected to fertilize the neural connections necessary to experience life through new eyes. Newberg's discoveries, along with the findings of Dr. Richard J. Davidson, show us why meditation is so beneficial to us: it activates the areas of the brain associated with higher consciousness, enhanced attention, and feelings of joy, happiness, and compassion.

Most people are familiar with the stress-reducing benefits of meditation, and everyone would like to experience heightened attention and greater joy in their life. Yet most people do not meditate because they claim to be "too busy" and do not have the time to sit down and meditate for twenty minutes. But what if we began with a one-minute meditation that was incredibly effective and did not interfere with our daily activities?

Before you begin the one-minute meditation, take a moment to close your eyes. Breathe and notice that each time you think, you tend to hold your breath. As you become aware that your thoughts stop your breath, your awareness will automatically restart your natural breathing cycle. As you begin to breathe again, you reestablish your natural state of flow. You are either thinking or breathing. Thinking feeds the mind and starves the body. Breathing calms the mind, inspires and feeds life into the body.

The process of *getting out of our head* begins with noticing the inverse relationship between breathing and thinking. When breathing is "on," thinking is "off," and vice versa. The continual expansion and contraction associated with breathing is how the primal rhythm of life expresses itself within the body.

What we call a thought is nothing more than an impermanent expression of consciousness, a momentary wave in the ocean of life. When we focus on that fleeting manifestation, forgetting that we are its observer, we find ourselves entangled in its web. As we become aware of that web, however, the truth of that awareness sets us free.

Just as a classroom filled with noisy students quiets under the gaze of their teacher, the power of our own awareness eventually paves the way for our liberation. The One-Minute Breath Meditation below will help you to see beyond the mind's distractions to the clarity and spaciousness of your true nature.

Usually we refer to activities such as this as *techniques* or *exercises*, and we believe that practicing them over and over again is what creates change. But I have not found that to be true. From my experience, repetition does not create the change but rather the fact that we see something in a new way. The awareness is curative, as I pointed out in the last chapter. If it takes effort to create change, it will take effort to maintain it. And if it takes effort to maintain it, it probably will not be maintained, because the body is designed to take the path of least resistance.

THE ONE-MINUTE BREATH MEDITATION

Week 1

Tonight, when you lie down in bed, take a minute to close your eyes and notice how your chest expands and contracts. Each time you notice a thought or some inner dialogue, allow that awareness to automatically bring you back to your breath. Continue noticing your breath until you naturally fall asleep.

If you awaken during the night to use the bathroom, sit on the toilet (even if you normally stand up), close your eyes, and just watch your breath. When you return to bed, continue noticing your breath until you fall asleep again. Anytime you awaken during the night or find it difficult to sleep, just observe your breath, knowing that anytime a thought arises, awareness will automatically guide you back to your breath.

Upon awakening, close your eyes for a minute and once again notice your breath until you feel ready to get up and start your day. Anytime you use the bathroom, sit down, close your eyes, notice your breath, notice your thoughts, and notice that you are the *noticer*. Watch your breath for approximately one minute before and after each meal, and anytime you feel anxious, worried, or overwhelmed. Notice it when you are on the subway and during the day, whenever you feel the urge to do so. There is no need to keep a count. But if possible, repeat this process whenever it enters your awareness.

Week 2

After integrating the One-Minute Breath Meditation into your daily routine for a week, you may wish to decrease the length of your meditation to about thirty seconds, while increasing how often you do it. Although the idea of doing something throughout the day sounds difficult, it is actually very easy because you are not doing anything other than noticing your breath. Continue this *noticing* until awareness of your breath is as natural as breathing itself.

Week 3

After noticing your breath for two weeks, try it with your eyes open while brushing your teeth, eating a meal, watching TV, taking a walk, and especially while driving your car. Watch your breath from the time you pull out of your driveway until you get to the end of the block. Then begin again, noticing your breath until you get to the traffic light three blocks away. Now watch your breath until the song on the radio ends, until you get to the next stop sign or the entrance to the freeway.

Within a few weeks of integrating breath awareness into your own life, it will begin to feel so natural that you may find yourself losing track of time and forgetting how often you do it or for how long. As these brief gaps of time link up, extended periods of spaciousness arise where the mind empties and the outside world disappears. Heaven and earth become one, and all that remains is the inherent peace and spaciousness of just *being*.

Awareness in Action

In early theatrical productions, actors would use handheld masks to create desired personas. The real people, however, were not visible but rather always peering through their masks. The word *person* is derived from the Latin *personare*, which means "to sound through." In other words, the person is not the mask or the persona but the *essence* that expresses itself through it. Most of us confuse our true essence, the *witness*, with the ongoing chatter created by the conscious mind's persona.

The One-Minute Arrow Meditation below will allow you to directly notice how this false identity interferes with your ability to breathe freely, learn effortlessly, and experience true presence. As the One-Minute Arrow Meditation becomes an integral part of your daily routine, continue with the One-Minute Breath Meditation previously discussed.

THE ONE-MINUTE ARROW MEDITATION

To get started, gather a large piece of poster board and a few markers. Create an arrow chart like the one below. When finished, attach the chart to a wall or door so that it is at eye level. Make sure there is enough space in front of the chart for you to move closer or farther away from it as necessary. If you wear glasses and feel comfortable without them, please remove them. Stand close enough to the chart to see it comfortably.

Begin each meditation with the upper left-hand arrow. Stand with your knees slightly bent and remember to breathe gently throughout. These meditations are done for approximately one minute and can be repeated as often as you like.

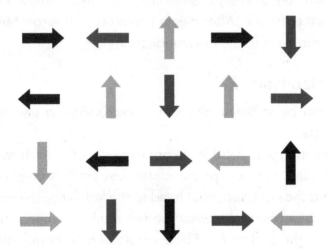

Arrow Meditation 1

1. Begin by looking at the first arrow in the upper left-hand corner. Slowly turn your head and eyes in the direction the arrow is pointing and then back to center. Use your breath to guide your movement, for example, *inhale*, gently turning your head in the direction of the arrow...*exhale*, returning your head to center.

2. Now inhale and turn your head in the direction the second arrow is pointing. After you have turned your head as far as it can comfortably go without strain or effort, exhale and return back to center.

3. Continue to turn your head, along with your eyes, in the direction of each arrow until you reach the end of the chart. Remember to breathe throughout.

If you begin to think, lose your place, or feel confused, just close your eyes, breathe gently, and begin again at the first arrow in the upper left-hand corner. Continue doing the One-Minute Arrow Meditation a few times a day until you are able to smoothly turn your head, along with your eyes, from one arrow to the next without stopping or holding your breath. If you are able to easily see the chart, feel free to move back a little farther from it. After gaining comfort with Arrow Meditation 1, move on to the next meditation.

Arrow Meditation 2

1. Begin by softening the knees and breathing gently and slowly.

2. Then turn your head in the opposite direction each arrow is pointing. For example, since the first arrow is pointing toward the right, turn your head to the left. Since the second arrow is pointing toward the left, turn your head toward the right, and so on. For example, *inhale*, gently turning

your head in the opposite direction of the arrow…*exhale*, returning your head to center.

As you begin this version of the arrow meditation, are you feeling unsure of yourself or feeling a need to rehearse internally? If so, close your eyes, breathe, and when you are ready, begin again with the first arrow in the upper left-hand corner. Continue doing this meditation several times a day until you are able to easily turn your head, along with your eyes, from one arrow to the next without stopping or interfering with your breath.

Arrow Meditation 3

1. Begin with gentle breathing and softened knees, as in the earlier meditations.
2. This time, simply call out the direction of each arrow instead of turning your head. For example, with a soft gaze upon the arrow chart, *inhale*, breathing…*exhale*, "right"… *inhale*, breathing…*exhale*, "left," and so on.

If you notice any tension or mental distractions, close your eyes and take a deep breath. When you feel ready, begin again with the first arrow. Once you are able to repeatedly flow through this meditation easily, you may move on to the next one.

Arrow Meditation 4

1. Stand at a comfortable distance in front of the arrow chart. Slowly inhale and exhale and gaze softly at the chart, keeping your knees slightly bent.
2. As you follow your breath, call out the opposite direction each arrow is pointing. For example, since the first arrow is pointing toward the right, you will say "left." Since

the second arrow is pointing toward the left, you will say "right," and so on.

Remember to go slowly, and if you get distracted, close your eyes, take a deep breath, and begin again with the first arrow. If you have other things on your mind, feel free to do the meditation when you feel more at ease.

Arrow Meditation 5

1. Begin as usual, as in Arrow Meditation 4.
2. Following your breath, call out the direction of each arrow while simultaneously moving both palms in the direction of the arrow. For example, since the first arrow is pointing right, you will say "right" while moving your palms toward the right, and so on.

Remember to move slowly and breathe rhythmically as if you are moving in slow motion. If you get distracted, close your eyes, take a breath, and begin again with the first arrow. Feel free to move farther away from the chart, as long as you are able to easily see it without effort.

Arrow Meditation 6

1. Stand at a comfortable distance in front of the arrow chart, and notice your breathing as you stand with a slight bend in the knees and a softened gaze.
2. This time, call out the direction of each arrow, while simultaneously moving both palms in the opposite direction. For example, since the first arrow is pointing right, you will say "right" while moving your palms toward the left. Since the second arrow is pointing toward the left, you will say "left" while moving your palms to the right, and so on. If you stumble, pause, breathe, and begin again.

This meditation will probably feel very confusing at first, so go slowly, allowing each movement to unfold on its own. As you move from one arrow to the next, continue the process until everything smooths out. Once this occurs, your breath will flow, your mind will quiet, your mouth will speak, and your arms will move with no effort on your part.

If you wish to take this process a bit further, you may follow along with the meditation below.

Arrow Meditation 7

1. Begin as usual with gentle breathing and a softened gaze, as you stand at a comfortable distance in front of the arrow chart.
2. Move both hands in the direction of each arrow, while calling out the opposite. For example, since the first arrow is pointing right, you will move your hands to the right while saying "left." Since the second arrow is pointing toward the left, you will move your hands toward the left while saying "right."
3. When you are able to do this variation smoothly and accurately, then alternate between Arrow Meditations 6 and 7. First go through the entire chart, calling out the direction of each arrow while moving your hands in the opposite direction. Then go through the chart moving your hands in the direction of each arrow while saying the opposite. Switch back and forth between these two variations until you are able to easily flow from one variation to the other.

By doing the One-Minute Arrow Meditation, we quickly notice the mental strategies that constrict our breath, steal our flow, and cripple our ability to learn without effort and experience true presence. When our breath is full, our mind is quiet and we *flow*. When our breath is shallow, our mind is active and we *slow*. The purpose of these meditations is to notice what causes our breath to stop, and how the simple act of noticing starts it again.

No matter what we are involved in, the body is always expanding and contracting. Our lungs are continuously inflating and deflating. And our breath is an expression of this rhythmic pulse of life. It is not us breathing; it is life breathing us.

Years ago I shared this work with a young man who has now become a successful actor and singer and who also mentors young performers. This was his experience:

> Working with the arrow meditation confronted me with the kind of fear I have faced during high-level performance experiences — that sense of "I don't know what I'm doing, I don't even know how to approach this" — and it gave me a chance to face that fear without the burden of "trying." For it was "trying," I later learned, that had fooled me into believing I wasn't already the target I wished to reach.
>
> I remember a sense of something deeper taking over during the exercises, which transcended the realm of "trying," dropping me into a kind of deep learning — some might call it "the zone." To me, it felt like a kind of fluidity, which seemed to hum or vibrate.
>
> In sharing my adaptation of this work with students, it allowed them a firsthand experience of presence — presence despite whatever (apparently) difficult task confronted them. This gave them direct knowledge that the seat of all performance — of all being, in fact — was how deeply they could remain embodied and in touch with their breath. They realized that there was a kind of safety, even in the face of "risk," when they didn't leave themselves and hide behind their minds.

This work is hard to talk about because it dips beneath rational understanding into inspired action. It's the most effective tool I've encountered for experiencing effortless mastery.

Living in "the Zone"

There is a major difference between our ideas about life and life itself. It is one thing to experience peace in a meditation retreat, and another to maintain it in the midst of life's everyday challenges. Staying in "the zone" during our everyday life is the difference between average existence and a life filled with peace and passion. It is a skill that can be developed and expanded. First, however, we must uncover what habitually takes us out of the zone, diminishing our ability to see and experience presence.

The most peaceful part of our twenty-four-hour daily living cycle is when we fall asleep at night. For many of us, the last sound we make before falling asleep is a sigh of relief. That sigh is our way of saying the struggle is over. The worries, concerns, and challenges of the day are put aside, and we can finally rest because our mind is quiet. Wouldn't it be nice if we could access that same feeling during the day? We can! But we must realize that whatever we identify with is what is real for us. If we identify with the habitual chatter, worry, and concern of the conscious mind, then that becomes our reality and what occupies our life. If, however, we realize that we are actually the *silent peaceful witness*, then that becomes our reality and life takes on a different flavor.

We have been taught that our ability to think is our prime attribute. But each time we interact with the mind seeking meaning, understanding, and control of our lives, we rob ourselves of the opportunity to experience profound peace, the kind of serenity that comes from realizing that everything in the universe is taking care of itself. Everything that needs to happen happens exactly when it needs to because the intelligence of life is guiding our every move. Our real healing comes from the unconditional acceptance that accompanies this realization.

By using the one-minute meditations shared in this chapter, we will discover not only how to enter "the zone" but also how to live there. Next I will discuss how the intelligence of life brings us the precise experiences necessary to spur the process of evolution. Get ready for the real *law of attraction*.

CHAPTER TEN

The True Law of Attraction

One does not become enlightened by imagining figures of light,
but by making the darkness conscious. The latter procedure, however,
is disagreeable and therefore not popular.

—— CARL JUNG

*A*round 400 BCE, Hippocrates, the father of Western medicine, said, "By similar things a disease is produced and through the application of the like is cured." In the sixteenth century, Paracelsus, the first physician to note that some diseases are rooted in psychological illness, declared that small doses of "what makes a man ill also cures him." Although this principle is foundational to the science of homeopathy created by Samuel Hahnemann in 1796, I believe that Hippocrates and Paracelsus were actually describing one of nature's fundamental principles of healing, which became evident to them while observing the dynamics of their own lives and those of others.

Just as every human being has a unique identifying fingerprint, each chemical element in the periodic table of elements also emits a distinctive spectral fingerprint. These characteristically colored bands, known as Fraunhofer lines, can be observed through a spectroscope when an element is heated into an excited state. When that same element is cooled and exposed to a light source such as the sun, it will absorb from the source the identical spectral fingerprint emitted when it was excited.

For example, when hydrogen gas is heated it emits a set of visible spectral lines seen as colored bands. However, if sunlight interacts with hydrogen gas that is cool, the hydrogen will absorb light energy in the exact same locations as when it was heated.

All elements in an environment of light attract to themselves precisely the light energy they emit when excited. This is significant, when you consider that the entire mass of the human body is composed of a vast multitude of elements in a dynamic state, and that we live on a planet suffused with light. It means we are constantly emitting an energetic fingerprint of colored light that is attracting to itself a mirror image of that energy. This is the true *law of attraction*. What we emit is what we attract, and what we attract is what we need, but not necessarily what we want or desire.

To see how this concept applies to our everyday lives, consider the possibility that life continually provides us with experiences that act as potent homeopathic remedies designed to rouse and bring to awareness what we need to heal and grow. Thus, the events and individuals in our life are actually evolutionary remedies that continually reflect to us what requires our attention, distilling from our state of consciousness its desire for wellness on all levels. Although the incidents we reject usually result in emotionally charged allergic reactions, those reactions can become a beacon for healing, attracting to us precisely what we need to embrace to spur our development. As the ancient sages said, "Crisis leads to opportunity." Little did I know of that reality as a young man, when my life came crashing down on me.

The Science of Life

In December 1977 my marriage suddenly fell apart. This led to a painful divorce, and like many who are faced with the shock of an unexpected and inexplicable loss, I broke down. For the next six years I suffered from severe panic attacks every day throughout the day. Nearly incapacitated by them, I began seeing a therapist who asked a question that eventually transformed my understanding of my life and how I care for others: What did this breakup teach you about your relationship with your wife?

My answer: I married my father, dressed as a woman.

My father had loved me, but he had also been a very critical person who was unable to share what he was feeling. For example, upon my graduation from optometry school as one of the top ten students in my class, he asked, "Why didn't you become an ophthalmologist?"

My wife was not critical in the same way as my father. However, she was unable to share what she was feeling, resulting in a similar relational dynamic at the time (she is now one of my closest friends). If she was upset about something but unable to share it, I would respond the same way I had responded to my father: by feeling misunderstood. It was the same pattern.

Then, as I looked back over my life, I understood that my wife was not my only father-in-disguise. I had had similar relational dynamics with intimate partners before her, and the same was true of my closest male friends, employers, and most of my teachers in school. Unresolved issues with my father kept resurfacing.

It was as if my friends, lovers, and teachers were somehow conspiring to activate and heal those early psychological wounds. I realized that my life was not just a series of random events. It was just the opposite. It was a synchronized (and seemingly magnetic) process in which the precise experiences and people needed to facilitate my healing were attracted to me. This discovery not only transformed my life but also led to the therapeutic technique I will share with you in the next chapter.

The long and very difficult period after my divorce made me realize that the road to wellness is often bumpy. According to psychologist and author Rollo May, "One does not become fully human painlessly." We have an opportunity to embrace each situation with an open heart, recognizing that encountering disturbance and obstacles in one's life is not necessarily problematic. A grain of sand irritating an oyster creates a pearl. Whether we are discussing physics, chemistry, or human interactions, disruption is the catalyst that often brings change. Electrons jump to a higher orbit when they are perturbed. Chemical reactions occur when homeostasis or stability is disturbed. And human beings often transform themselves when they are stressed. We cannot even wash our clothes without agitation.

Human Homeopathy

Perhaps, like me, you have noticed a certain type of person who keeps appearing in your life. Maybe it is a parental figure who seemed to be absent during your childhood or that bully from seventh grade, the one who ridiculed you and brought out a feeling of being small and unprotected.

At some point, that specific person may have dropped out of your life but, if an important issue was not fully resolved with that person, someone with the same personality seems to reappear. As a result, you have gone from relationship to relationship, job to job, and life experience to life experience feeling as if you are being followed. No matter where you go, the same experiences occur over and over again. Or, to quote the popular saying, "Wherever you go, there you are."

Usually we try to avoid people who upset us. Yet in most cases, no matter where we turn, there they are. Eventually it becomes clear that there is nowhere to run or hide. Our only option is to embrace them as part of the cure because the people who trigger our pain are actually a blessing in disguise. By pushing our buttons, they bring things to the surface, helping us to open up, become aware, and heal ourselves so as to experience more of what life has to offer.

I call this *human homeopathy*. Homeopathy is a system of alternative medicine in which *like cures like*. In essence, the same substance that causes our symptoms is the one that ultimately is part of the cure; the remedy is energetically identical to its affliction. In human homeopathy, we experience allergic reactions to certain types of people and experiences. Until now, when you encountered one of these situations and the allergic reaction that ensued, you probably pushed it away or tried to calm yourself with distraction. The moment we experience something in life that triggers sensitivity or reaction, the mind automatically tries to change the subject or withdraw as a way of protecting us from uncomfortable feelings. However, there is an alternative: accepting and embracing the allergen. Right now, you may have one or more allergies to life situations and people, and when encountered, these allergies take you from a state of ease to a state of dis-ease. If ignored, dis-ease can become the foundation for disease. As in the practice of medical homeopathy, the answer is not avoidance. It is gently embracing the situation or person until you are able to naturally accept its therapeutic value.

We can learn a great deal about life by noticing how the roots of a tree deal with obstacles. When roots encounter rocks obstructing their passage, they usually encircle the rocks and embrace them, transforming an impediment into an advantage that ultimately strengthens their foundation. The same is also true of our own lives. As we embrace the miraculous intelligence of life, our roots deepen, providing a sense of fluid stability that keeps us poised and directed even in the presence of strong winds.

"But," you may be thinking, "I don't want to embrace the difficult people or situations in my life!" Of course you don't, and you don't have to. Instead, you can acknowledge what they represent, which is actually a much gentler approach that allows that tension to dissipate on its own. I call this process *color homeopathy*.

Color Homeopathy

Although I have used color therapeutically since 1971, I was first introduced to an entire system of color therapy called *syntonics* in 1977 by my dear friend and colleague Dr. Larry Jebrock. Syntonics involves the application of colored light through the eyes to rebalance areas of the brain affecting visual function. After using syntonics on a dozen patients with vision problems, I found that the results were so profound that I conducted three pilot studies of my own to evaluate what other functions might be affected by light's coloration.

I began by exposing my patients to all the colors of the rainbow to see how certain colors affected not only their vision but also their moods and performance. For example, if someone had too much heat — perhaps in the form of a fever or inflammation or figuratively in the form of anger — I would treat them with cooling colors, exposing them to blue-green light to calm an inflammation, lower their temperature, and soothe their distress. If their issues stemmed from lack of heat — they were pale and suffering from a chronic condition — I exposed them to warming yellow-green colors, which increased their energy and vitality.

The data gathered during the final study, which became the basis of my PhD dissertation, demonstrated that syntonics increases attention, learning, and memory. It also proved valuable in the treatment of migraine headaches, pain, and inflammation of the eyes, as well as head trauma. However, its major benefit was its ability to expand a person's visual field (how much a person is able to see peripherally while looking straight ahead) and visual memory (a person's ability to remember what they have seen). The expansion of your visual field not only is critical to a more effortless way of seeing, but also dramatically affects your entire perspective, allowing you to see life as a whole rather than through a hole.

In the process of conducting this research I also found that color was inseparably linked to our emotions. Different people reacted to the same colors in different ways. Each person seemed comfortable with some colors and uncomfortable with others.

So I started asking patients which colors they liked and disliked. When I exposed them briefly to the colors they did not like, it evoked a subtle (and sometimes not so subtle) agitation, causing the patient to release feelings of sadness or other emotions that traced back to unsettling experiences. Other colors brought them joy, a sense of safety, and comfort. It was as if they had an allergic reaction to certain colors because those colors awakened old painful memories and the feelings that accompanied them. As Rumi tells us, "The wound is the place where the Light enters you."

The idea of human homeopathy kept coming to me. I began asking my patients about their lives and, sure enough, there was a definite correlation between specific colors and sensitive issues in their lives. Even for me, when I viewed indigo light, a panic attack immediately came on, triggering memories of painful experiences with my father. I wondered, were small doses of indigo what I needed to heal?

So I tried something different. I initially observed the colors I felt comfortable with and then gradually exposed myself to small, gentle doses of the colors that made me uncomfortable. The results were so powerful that I repeated the same process with my patients. What I discovered was fascinating. Becoming receptive to the full spectrum of light not only expanded my patients' field of vision but also granted them access to feelings, memories, and other aspects of life they were previously unaware of. Once their perception widened, many of my patients reported having spontaneous insights. Some even reported precognitive visions, affording them a glimpse of events that later occurred. It soon became obvious that as we become receptive to the full spectrum of light, we are simultaneously able to embrace the full spectrum of life.

How does color homeopathy do this? Colored light slips beneath our conscious awareness, reaching beyond the cerebral cortex and into the primitive brainstem that controls our innate response to color. It penetrates our emotional and memory centers while triggering significant psychophysiological responses. In bringing unresolved issues to conscious awareness, color homeopathy unearths the emotional roots of our visual field constriction, ultimately freeing us from our past trauma.

Could psychotherapy accomplish the same thing? Possibly, but based on my clinical experience using color homeopathically, viewing colored light can often access deep issues much faster. Psychology works at the speed of life. Color homeopathy works at the speed of light, and its effect cannot be blocked with emotional resistance. As soon as you observe a certain color, there is an association. It is a primal experience.

Color is color, you might think. What does a color have to do with how I feel? If you ask a physicist about the nature of reality and the foundation of life, they will tell you that everything in life — everything you see, hear, feel, taste, and touch — is a vibration. Take any object. Yes, it seems solid until you put it under a microscope. Continue to magnify what you see and eventually all that remains is its vibrational signature. At the most fundamental level, the real underpinning of reality is the vibration of light. Color is just our visual perception of light vibrating at specific frequencies.

Just as some life experiences are easy for us to accept and others are difficult, the energetic frequencies that compose these experiences are likewise either comfortable or uncomfortable for us to embrace. We respond to specific colors in the same way we respond to specific life experiences. But it is not the color we are responding to but rather the vibration that we interpret as color. And even our interpretation of color can be radically different than someone else's interpretation. Your red could be someone else's blue. But even if you perceive a color differently, it will not affect the way you feel about it.

According to Jay Neitz, a professor of ophthalmology at the

University of Washington, most scientists previously thought that people with normal vision saw colors similarly because their perceptions of color were linked to universal emotional responses. But now that has changed.

In research published in the journal *Nature* in 2009, Neitz and his colleagues injected the eyes of monkeys, who were naturally sensitive to just green and blue, with a virus that gave some of their green-sensing cones the ability to also see red. Even though the monkeys' brains were innately wired to perceive only green and blue, they spontaneously adapted, enabling them to also see red. The results of this research indicate that wavelengths have no predetermined perceptions. In other words, we each have a unique perception of color, or our own color spectrum.

According to Professor Fritz-Albert Popp, pioneer in biophotonic research, "We are still on the threshold of fully understanding the complex relationship between light and life, but we can now say emphatically that the function of our entire metabolism is dependent on light." Since light is composed of different wavelengths that we perceive as color, the way we metabolize color is inseparable from the way we metabolize life. As we embrace the full spectrum of light, we embrace the full spectrum of life.

CHAPTER ELEVEN

Full-Spectrum Life

When all things are seen equally, the timeless Self-essence is reached.
— Seng-Ts'an, Third Zen Patriarch

A seamless connection exists between light and life. Frequencies of light, perceived by us as color, can trigger specific thoughts, feelings, and emotions in the same way that certain life experiences do. As our receptivity to the visible spectrum of light increases, so too does our ability to live a more vibrant and colorful life. Thus, colored light has the power to unlock our potential and liberate our inherent luminosity.

To experience this dynamic connection, let me guide you through a short visualization. You might find it useful to have a notebook nearby on which to jot down your observations. Or some people like to use a voice recorder. Either way, read through the following visualization once, and then try it with your eyes closed.

THE COLOR DOME VISUALIZATION

Imagine that you are sitting comfortably inside a large translucent dome that allows the sun to shine through, bathing you in soft, pure light. Now imagine a small dial that allows you to gradually increase the brightness of the light until you find the level that is most comfortable for you. As you breathe in, imagine yourself filling up with this pure light, and notice how you feel.

Is this a comfortable sensation for you? Does your breathing or heart rate change in any way as you take in the light? Are you at ease, or do any feelings, images, or memories come to mind? Do you wish to linger or move on? When you feel ready, take a few breaths and then jot down anything you noticed about your experience.

Now imagine that you have the option to change the color of the dome to red. How do you feel about that? Are you looking forward to seeing the red? Apprehensive? Neutral? Or would you prefer to go on to the orange dome? Follow your intuition and do what feels most comfortable.

If you decide to bypass the red dome and go to the orange, make a note that you are bypassing red. However, if you decide to experience the red, imagine the dome filled with soft red light. Use the imaginary dial to gradually increase the intensity of the color until you find the most comfortable level. Now breathe in the red and see how it feels. Notice any physical sensations, emotions, or memories that come to the surface.

Stay in the red dome as long as you like. And when you are ready, imagine the dome returning once again to the soft, pure light that we began with. Now take a few deep breaths and jot down anything you noticed about your response to red.

Continue in this way, experiencing all the other colors of the rainbow: orange, yellow, green, blue, indigo (deep blue, like the bottom of the ocean), and violet. Explore each color thoroughly, and stay as long or as little as you like, or even skip some colors altogether. Remember to record the physical sensations, feelings, reactions, or memories that arise with each color.

Understanding the Color Visualization

The visualization I just described can be powerful, and everyone's response is unique. Some people weep when they imagine certain colors. Others tell me one color brings deep comfort and joy, while another stirs up sorrow. Still other people experience immediate, visceral anxiety or anger as soon as they start to imagine one color or another. And some people feel so averse to some colors that they cannot bring themselves to imagine them at all. These reactions offer valuable insights into our inner emotional terrain. They allow us a glimpse deep into the psyche.

Not long ago I mentored Walter, a retired medical school professor who had serious vision problems associated with his diabetes. During our initial consultation he told me that at the age of eight he found out that he had an older brother who had mysteriously drowned when he (Walter) was less than three years old. Shortly after he found this out, he developed issues with his heart and was then diagnosed with type 1 diabetes. According to Walter, the mystery surrounding his brother's death had haunted him since childhood.

This is what he reported as we did the color visualization.

Pure Light: "I'm not entirely comfortable. Apprehensive. I can't see a clear picture."

Red: "This feels anxious. Threatening. Uncomfortable. Apprehensive. That's how I felt when I saw that look on my mother's face."

Orange: "It's pleasant. It's not like red, but my mind seems to be changing a lot. This is not a color that will take me anywhere. I am just there. It's just okay."

Yellow: "This reminds me of a warm bath. It's better than orange. It's pleasing. I feel alive and energized. I'm at home."

Green: "I have to step back. This feels lethargic. It's heavy. There's pain and depression. I grew up around this."

Blue: "This is a healing color. I am breathing easier. But my father is present and he's interfering with my healing. Now I see my mother again. She's a source of anxiety."

Indigo: "This feels inviting. Now I have mixed feelings. I want to make it pure blue, not indigo blue. I keep changing the color because it's bringing up anxiety, even more anxiety than red. It's reminding me of my brother drowning. My mother never let me go in the ocean after that because she was afraid I would drown too."

Violet: "This is a very good feeling. It's reassuring and healing."

All that insight came up over the phone with a man I had never previously spoken with. Imagine how much psychotherapy would be needed to uncover what arose with just a five-minute visualization!

Take a moment now and review the notes you took about your experience with each color. Which colors brought you peace, warmth, and joy? Which ones felt uncomfortable, leading you to recoil, stop what you were doing, or become anxious or sad? Which ones did you avoid, rush through, or skip altogether?

The colors you recoiled from represent the portions of the visible spectrum that you are sensitive or "allergic" to. When you are averse to a certain color, such as red, you will do your best to avoid the spectrum of light that you perceive as red, as well as the spectrum of life that corresponds to red. Let me explain what I mean.

Imagine that from the moment of your birth, every experience of your life was filmed. Now imagine that you are going to watch that movie. After finding a comfortable seat in the theater, you are hooked up to a series of biofeedback monitors that record your responses to everything you see. The scenes that reflect joyful times entrain your breathing, blood pressure, and brain waves into a balanced, peaceful state. In the process, you relax and your field of vision expands, allowing you to see and experience more.

Conversely, scenes that reflect unpleasant events constrict your breath, tighten your muscles, accelerate your heart rate, and disturb your emotions. In addition, they diminish your field of vision, literally shutting out a portion of what you see, reducing your capacity to receive and embrace life with ease. Even though the events on the screen are merely projections of light and are not, in fact, happening in real time, your body responds with *receptivity* or *rejection*, based on the emotions they stir in you.

Just as some experiences are easier to accept than others, the colors that energetically match these experiences will also be comfortable or uncomfortable to look at. So if our receptivity to the color spectrum is limited, the amount of light and life that we are able to receive will also be limited. As we gradually desensitize ourselves from the allergic reactions to these colors, we will begin to experience more openness and receptivity to life.

If you think of each color as a room in a seven-bedroom home, then it is easy to see that, in Walter's case, there were only two rooms — the yellow and the violet room — where he felt at home. He only occasionally visited the other rooms, or avoided them altogether, because they triggered deep anxieties that stemmed from childhood memories.

Perhaps in your home things are much the same. You have seven rooms, but you are restricting yourself to just one or two of them. How would it be if you felt comfortable in every single room?

Consider how expansive life would be if you felt "at home" in every area of your life.

With the aid of color homeopathy, you will be able to gradually embrace the colors you once recoiled from, outgrowing your allergy to them and, more importantly, your aversion to the people and experiences those colors represent in your life. In Walter's case, after he confronted the painful memories that certain colors brought up, he experienced greater comfort because he was able to fill in some of the blanks surrounding his brother's drowning. As a result, his eyesight improved and the insights he gained finally allowed him to put the mystery to rest.

Now let's try another visualization that will help reveal how our color allergies relate to our health and wellness. You will need a pen or pencil and some paper for this exercise.

THE BODY MAP VISUALIZATION

Imagine you are naked and standing in front of a full-length mirror. While looking at your reflection, visually scan your body. Start at your feet and slowly move up, noting the areas of your body where you hold tension, have had infections, surgeries, injuries, chronic aches and pains, or suffered emotional trauma in the past. For example, if you tend to suffer from hay fever, perhaps your sinuses represent an area of the body that presents issues for you. Or maybe you have repeated bladder infections, headaches, back pain, or fertility issues. Now draw a simple picture of a body (a stick figure is fine) and circle all the areas that cause you problems or have a history of physical or emotional trauma. Then look at the chakra chart below and see how your physical issues and their corresponding chakras compare to the colors you are allergic to.

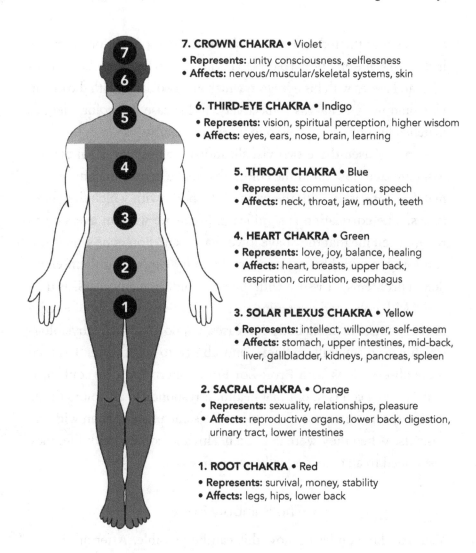

7. CROWN CHAKRA • Violet
• **Represents:** unity consciousness, selflessness
• **Affects:** nervous/muscular/skeletal systems, skin

6. THIRD-EYE CHAKRA • Indigo
• **Represents:** vision, spiritual perception, higher wisdom
• **Affects:** eyes, ears, nose, brain, learning

5. THROAT CHAKRA • Blue
• **Represents:** communication, speech
• **Affects:** neck, throat, jaw, mouth, teeth

4. HEART CHAKRA • Green
• **Represents:** love, joy, balance, healing
• **Affects:** heart, breasts, upper back, respiration, circulation, esophagus

3. SOLAR PLEXUS CHAKRA • Yellow
• **Represents:** intellect, willpower, self-esteem
• **Affects:** stomach, upper intestines, mid-back, liver, gallbladder, kidneys, pancreas, spleen

2. SACRAL CHAKRA • Orange
• **Represents:** sexuality, relationships, pleasure
• **Affects:** reproductive organs, lower back, digestion, urinary tract, lower intestines

1. ROOT CHAKRA • Red
• **Represents:** survival, money, stability
• **Affects:** legs, hips, lower back

The seven chakras

After using color homeopathy with thousands of individuals, I have noticed that most of the time their color allergies closely overlap with the areas of their body where they have had physical issues or injuries, or where they hold emotional stress. For example, Walter had a loss of feeling in his feet and issues with sexuality and digestion, which are related to the red and orange chakras. He also mentioned that he had taken some emotional blows to his heart, and he had arthritis in his neck and issues with his eyesight, which are associated with the green, blue, and indigo chakras respectively. In his case, his color allergies matched his physical and emotional issues exactly.

Having used these two visualizations for decades, I am continually amazed how often the colors that make people uncomfortable match up precisely with the parts of the body with which they have issues. The correlation is significant. Someone with an aversion to red may tell me that they have lower back pain. Someone who is uncomfortable with blue may report difficulty expressing themselves, dental problems, or issues with their thyroid. In many cases, as they work with color and overcome these "allergies," the flow of energy to those areas of their body increases, supporting their physiological function, overall wellness, and ability to heal. After I shared these observations with Professor Fritz-Albert Popp, he confirmed that "when a cell is in optimal health, it responds to all colors of the visible spectrum equally." I noticed the same phenomenon with my patients. When they were in good health and content with life, they responded to all colors equally and with ease.

The Rainbow Body

You may be wondering how this can be possible. After all, colors are just wavelengths of light vibrating at a specific frequency. Red, for example, vibrates at approximately 625 to 760 nanometers (one-billionth of a meter), whereas violet vibrates at approximately 380 to 435 nanometers.

According to philosopher and scientist Christopher Hills, author of *Nuclear Evolution: Discovery of the Rainbow Body*, the chakras are located at the site of the body's seven major endocrine glands. They are ignited by the seven colors of the visible spectrum and related to

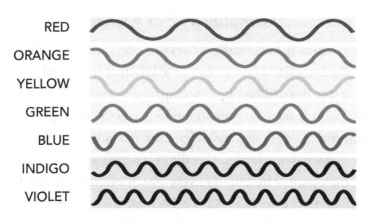

RED
ORANGE
YELLOW
GREEN
BLUE
INDIGO
VIOLET

Wavelengths of color

the attainment of health, happiness, and higher consciousness. Since the chakras are related not only to our physical health but also to our spiritual evolution, each one represents a unique aspect of our life's journey.

In light of this, I find it noteworthy that the third chakra, associated with the color yellow and described as the center of intellect, willpower, and self-esteem, comprises only 6.5 percent of the visible spectrum. Conversely, the first, sixth, and seventh chakras, associated with instinct, inner guidance, and a higher sense of knowing, respectively, comprise 84.2 percent of the visible spectrum. This significant difference further illustrates the relative contribution of our intellect and inner guidance to the unfolding of our consciousness.

Consciousness, like a prism, divides the invisible vibration called *light* into the visible vibrations we experience as color. Professor Popp noted that "when a cell is out of balance, it responds to colors of light selectively." Just as eating poorly results in malnutrition, not assimilating the full spectrum of light results in "mal-illumination." When our receptivity to the full spectrum of sunlight is lessened, our ability to function in total health and wellness is profoundly diminished.

Desensitizing Color Allergies

By systematically visualizing colors that feel uncomfortable, we can gradually desensitize ourselves to the habitual triggers that catalyze stress in our lives. Based on my clinical research and observations, colored light is the energetic foundation of our life experiences. By circumventing our conscious defenses, it provides us a clear glimpse of our deepest sensitivities. Gently visualizing specific colors, each at our own pace, can help us overcome these sensitivities to color — and therefore to life. As we become more comfortable with those colors, we will experience greater physical vitality, emotional well-being, and ease.

Here is how to do it. Once or twice a day for just a minute or two, go back to the color visualization dome. This time, however, just visit with each color, making each of them brighter or paler as needed. After you have taken in as much of one color as feels comfortable, move on to the next. You can go in any order you wish, at your own pace, so there is no need to give yourself more of a color than you can assimilate easily. Think of it as a meditation. In the privacy of your home, you get to relax inside your personal dome and dial in what you need. If you are feeling anxious and restless, you might calm down with a color you find soothing. If you are feeling grounded and centered, you might take a journey into the interior of your life, allowing color to catalyze a discovery about what is going on deep within the psyche.

You never have to feel overwhelmed. If a color is too much for you, simply imagine dialing it down to a comfortable level. Over time you will find that you can gradually increase the brightness and linger for longer periods, embracing the colors that initially felt uncomfortable.

Gauging Your Progress

As you overcome your sensitivity to certain colors and what they represent, your overall well-being will improve and a sense of peace and spaciousness will permeate your life, supplanting the emotional sensitivities that previously triggered you. From time to time, however, you may wish to evaluate your progress and see if you can benefit from working further with a specific color. To do so, use the following visualization.

THE LIGHT TANK VISUALIZATION

Imagine seven transparent cylindrical holding tanks in your body, arranged side by side, one right next to the other (as pictured on the next page). The first tank holds red, the next orange, the next yellow, and so on through green, blue, indigo, and violet. Now imagine a beam of light entering your eyes and passing through the prism of consciousness, where it is divided into seven rivers of liquid light — red, orange, yellow, green, blue, indigo, and violet — each flowing into its respective holding tank. Now look at each tank and note how full it is.

You may notice that some tanks may be full, others empty, and others in between those two extremes. Do you notice any change in your ability to hold more of the colors you were initially unable to embrace?

As you desensitize yourself to the colors that once felt uncomfortable and the feelings and memories they awaken, all your chakras will open, allowing your mind to relax, your health to improve, and your awareness to expand naturally. This is when life becomes a living meditation because light passes through you as if you were transparent. Rather than

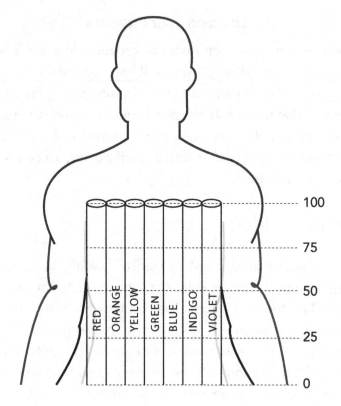

The Light Tank Visualization

feeling as if you are chronically bracing against uncomfortable experiences that might happen, you spontaneously see and respond to each situation as it occurs, allowing true *presence* to inhabit your life.

What Is Enlightenment?

When we think of enlightenment, we imagine a state of awakening absent of desire or suffering. We might envision someone meditating or providing spiritual insights to their followers. But enlightenment might just mean brightness — transparency — a luminous life.

Imagine a pure sheet of glass with no imperfections — nothing reflecting, distorting, or absorbing any of the light passing through it. Theoretically, when light moves through a pure piece of glass like that, 100 percent of the light is transmitted as if the glass did not exist. But if the glass contains any imperfections, it will alter the quantity and quality of the light moving through it.

We are each like a piece of perfectly clear glass with the potential to transmit all the light traversing our being. However, our ideas about life act like optical imperfections that can obscure our natural transparency. How we perceive life determines how effortlessly light passes through us. As the mind empties, however, our ideas disappear and all that remains is the pure light that we are.

The Hebrew Bible states that God initiated creation with the words, "Let there be light" (Genesis 1:3) — but it was not until three days after creation that God brought forth "lights in the firmament of the heaven to divide the day from the night" (Genesis 1:14). Based on the Bible's narrative, there is obviously a difference between the visible light of the sun, moon, and stars created on the fourth day, and the invisible light of the first day — the light of creation, the *intelligence of life.*

Light and life are two expressions of the same essence. Merging with the light of creation means that we are able to welcome the full spectrum of light *and* the full spectrum of life. Perhaps our lives are a journey guided by light, in which consciousness expands until it becomes one with the light that created it.

Becoming Light

When I sold my practice many years ago, I was asked why I did not keep any of my equipment. I responded by saying that I felt like I could do everything I needed with my heart and my hands. The person then asked me why I did not take my light machine, to which I replied, "You use the light until you see the light. And once you see the light, you become the light."

When the sun rises, flowers turn and grow toward it, absorbing its rays. As the sun sets, flowers gradually retreat and rest, preparing themselves for the next day, the next level of their evolvement. Humans respond the same way. We awaken to the light of day, continually align ourselves with the light, and finally retreat and rest, preparing ourselves for the next step of our life's journey.

Creation is the transformation of light into matter, and enlightenment is the return of matter back into light. Our physical life's journey begins with the materialization of spirit and ends with the spiritualization of matter. Our consciousness determines what frequencies of the light spectrum we are able to absorb. Those frequencies spiritualize matter into energy, causing us to glow. As consciousness expands, so does our glow. The frequencies of light that we are not yet able to absorb are reflected, attracting back to us matching life experiences that gradually help us embrace what previously disturbed us. When we are able to absorb the entire spectrum of light, "we" disappear and what remains is a holographic focal point of the sun.

CHAPTER TWELVE

Living in a World of Technology

Men have become the tools of their tools.
— HENRY DAVID THOREAU

Throughout this book I have discussed all the ways in which we are continually guided by light, the intelligence of life. In the last chapter I stated that our ability to embrace the full spectrum of light is directly related to our capacity to embrace the full spectrum of life. Yet life's intelligence, received through our inner guidance, is habitually interrupted or camouflaged by the mind's chatter.

A reflection of this same process is occurring worldwide, where we find ourselves in the midst of a highly magnified "technology takeover." The universal use of technology, much like our addiction to thinking, has resulted in a constant current of information interrupting the "flow" of our life. This intrusive pattern was initially marketed as "call-waiting" for our phones. But now our eyes, ears, and fingers are glued to our technology 24/7, searching for information on the web. We are bombarded by emails, texts, tweets, or the news feeds on our Facebook pages. My friend Ron refers to this technology as "weapons of mass distraction."

But how is this mass distraction affecting our degree of presence and ability to attend to the everyday demands of life? According to a 2010 Kaiser Family Foundation report, children from eight to eighteen spend an average of seven hours and thirty-eight minutes a day using entertainment media. At the same time, the Centers for Disease Control and Prevention report that the diagnosis of attention deficit hyperactivity disorder (ADHD) has continued to rise at an alarming rate for more than a decade. In addition, a study published in the August 2010 issue of *Pediatrics* found that exposure to screen media was associated with attention problems in a sample of 210 college students. But it does not stop there. According to the late Dr. Paul Pearsall, a psychoneuroimmunologist and *New York Times* bestselling author, all of us have become media frenzied and have developed a form of adult attention deficit disorder (AADD).

The distraction is just part of the larger picture. Dealing with a horde of daily text messages and emails makes it difficult for us to be by ourselves when all that activity stops. Although a sense of loneliness is natural at times, our addiction to the nonstop interaction afforded by technology amplifies that feeling when access to the technology is unexpectedly unavailable. Just think how you feel when you lack cell phone or web access. Is it possible that our obsession with continually checking our emails and text messages has contributed to our inability to genuinely relate with others and find contentment without constant stimulation?

Aside from the impact of technology on our attention and our ability to be at ease in the absence of our technology, let's examine how interacting with our devices interferes with the development of our fundamental communication and social skills. Many researchers observe that everyday conversation between human beings is becoming increasingly rare. Consider how often we speak to each other on the phone or have face-to-face conversations versus how often we communicate via text or email.

Those of us born before the age of computers and smartphones naturally developed these social skills because much of our life depended on directly communicating with each other. But all that has now changed, impacting our children in ways we cannot imagine. Many parents are so busy interacting with their handheld devices that they often give their children electronic games to soothe and entertain them instead of personally interacting with them. As a result, many of today's children are growing up with a built-in dependence on gadgetry, making it difficult for them to feel comfortable in everyday social situations. Often they find it challenging to make eye contact or deal with even the simplest face-to-face interactions without the aid of technology as an intermediary.

Over time these children forget how to relate with each other because they have become habituated to using technology to avoid direct contact with others and life itself. In fact, some neuroscientists believe that use of the internet actually rewires our brains.

We live in an age of information, but information is not wisdom. Information is transmitted from the head to the head. But wisdom is communicated by the heart. Wisdom comes from direct experience, and direct experience comes through interacting with each other and the world. During face-to-face interactions we transmit primal, nonverbal cues that subconsciously communicate critical information. These signals, transmitted through the eyes, facial expressions, body language, and pheromones, elicit instinctive responses that have evolved over millions of years. These highly evolved nonverbal communication skills allow us to function successfully in the world, and they only take place in the *presence* of each other.

The more we attach to technology, the less we bond with one another and the more we diminish our ability to cope with the everyday stressors of life. Unfortunately, we have become so dependent on our devices that many of us find it difficult to function if we are unplugged, even for a relatively short period.

In China, for instance, with its 1.2 billion cell phone users, the addiction to technology such as computer screens, cell phones, and video games has grown to such a degree that Chinese doctors consider it a clinical disorder. They have established a number of rehab centers where young people are completely isolated from all media. What is occurring in China is of particular relevance to American parents, who often give their young children cell phones or tablets to keep them quiet, and then notice those same children spending many hours glued to their electronic screens playing computer games, even when they take them on vacation, nature walks, or drives. In fact, in the fifth edition of the *Diagnostic and Statistical Manual of Mental Disorders* (DSM-5), internet gaming disorder is identified as a condition warranting more clinical research.

In 1978 I wrote the following in my journal: "It is the concept of time that is the cause of accidents, stress, and physical ailments. We developed this concept to improve our efficiency and control our destiny. Unfortunately, the monster we created is in constant competition with us and it is winning. If we didn't race against time, we wouldn't have accidents. If we didn't 'think ahead,' our organs wouldn't have to work so hard and break down as often. The clock now controls us." And I would update that today by saying it divorces us from the flow of *presence* available in each moment!

I had no idea back then how true those words were. But today it is not just our clocks. It's our computers, tablets, phones, the internet, and more. Technology that was designed to "save time" and assist us is now controlling us, looking after us, and looking over us all the time. There is hardly a place we can go where we will not be seen, photographed, or video-recorded. Our computers and phones have been promoted to being "personalized" and "smart," as they can predict what we want and give it to us, and we have been demoted to just being a "user." Did you notice that switch? Although our devices are "smart," we — as an expression of the grand intelligence of life — must remain aware of the benefits as well as the pitfalls of our technology, which can cut us off from this higher guidance.

We used to spend time with people face-to-face so we could look into their eyes and feel their presence. Now much of that has been replaced by emails, texts, and if we are lucky, video calls. We used to ask someone on a date when we felt a connection with them. Now we find our partners via online dating services that match us based on ideas and statistics about what people desire in others. We used to become intimately involved with another person if we felt some chemistry with them. Today, much of our sexuality is online with epidemic levels of sexting and internet porn. Whatever happened to timing and chemistry?

A computer now does almost everything we used to do manually — more efficiently. Most people used to know how to give change for a dollar. Now our cash registers tell us how much change we should give. What would we do if they did not compute that for us? Would we still be able to figure out how much change to give? We used to remember the phone numbers we most often called. Now we no longer need to exercise or develop our memory function because most calls are made by speed-dialing or asking Siri to dial the number for us. Many people today could not tell you their best friend's phone number if you asked them. Just as exercise is associated with maintaining health, using your memory is associated with preserving it. Doctors used to spend time with their patients, diagnosing and treating them by using their intuition and bedside manner along with their medical training. Today, evidence-based medicine with computerized symptom models often leaves little room for a doctor's unquantifiable wisdom and little time for them to get to know their patients.

As you can see, modern technology has very efficiently taken control of our lives. But it is only a reflection of the ego's proficiency in doing the same thing. The inner occupation by the virtual "me" is now echoed by technology everywhere we look. Is this called "creating our own reality"? If so, what is the value of this reality and how do we make use of the wonderful technology we have developed without injuring our health, happiness, and connection with nature?

Many years ago, when I was in optometry school, I was introduced to the concept of near-point stress. This occurs when our eyes are confined to a two-dimensional plane for prolonged periods while reading or computing, and is characterized by physiological changes associated with stress. The reason this occurs is that humans are genetically designed and neurologically wired to see the world in a three-dimensional form. Any activity or environment that creates a mismatch between our genetic design and our life's preoccupation creates stress, reducing our quality of life and potentially contributing to disease.

When your vision is confined, you feel imprisoned, as if you have lost your freedom. That can lead to a variety of stress-related symptoms and aberrant behaviors. Individuals who commit crimes are typically incarcerated in small cells without windows and given limited time outdoors. Violent criminals are confined in visually restricted solitary confinement for as much as twenty-three hours a day, where their eyes cannot escape confinement and see the light of day.

Restricting the expanse of our three-dimensional vision by focusing on our cell phones or computer monitors for extended periods is like being in an elevator for too long and wanting to escape. The human eye is primarily intended for distance vision. But since so much of our time is spent looking at our computer screens and cell phones, our eyes end up working too hard and, without frequent breaks, experience fatigue, which often leads to myopia and astigmatism.

Whenever you spend too much time focusing up close, you will notice that when you look up and away, things may initially appear blurry. That temporary blur at distance is one of the most common early symptoms of near-point stress that most people have experienced at some time in their lives. Other common symptoms of this stress syndrome include eyestrain, headaches, double vision, burning or watery eyes, and eyelid twitches.

As a result of the widespread use of computers and handheld devices, deteriorating vision is now the world's largest health epidemic and is continuously growing. Ian Morgan of Australian National University reported in the journal *Lancet* that up to 90 percent of young adults in China, Taiwan, Japan, Singapore, and South Korea are nearsighted. These statistics further confirm a 2009 National Eye Institute study that found an alarming 66 percent increase in the incidence of myopia in the United States since the early 1970s.

Scientists know that a person's environment is related to whether they develop myopia, and believe that staring at computer screens and cell phones is a major contributor to this epidemic. However, a new Australian study published in October 2015 has demonstrated that vision worsens in nearsighted children who spend less time outdoors. Based on the results of this study, the researchers recommend that children spend at least one to two hours per day outdoors to prevent nearsightedness or slow its progression.

Two-thirds of the US population wears glasses, yet less than 1 percent are born needing them. Virtually all Americans under age sixty use computers and as many as 90 percent complain about eyestrain (computer vision syndrome). These statistics are comparable to computer users in Europe. According to the International Telecommunication Union, there are almost as many cell phone subscriptions (6.8 billion) as there are people on this earth (7 billion).

This significant increase in the number of young people becoming myopic is quite telling. Just look through a pair of glasses used by a nearsighted person and you will notice that they make everything appear smaller and closer. The underlying reason for nearsightedness is that the person has literally shrunk their worldview in response to unnatural socially accepted demands, and the prescription in their glasses just mimics the perceptual adaptation they have made.

Since the use of computers and handheld devices significantly diminishes our field of perception, it is easy to see how the prolonged use of those technologies can cause a perceptual adaptation. The more we focus on digital technology at close distance, the more visual stress we create. And the more our perception narrows, the less we see, remember, and learn, resulting in less efficiency in our working lives, contrary to what the sellers of this technology tell us.

During a recent visit to New York City, I became aware of how modern technology was impacting our most fundamental human functions, including vision, hearing, sensitivity, health, and mortality. I was able to see the impact of this firsthand as I rode the subways. Most people were wearing earbuds as they focused on their smartphones, unconsciously compressing their peripheral vision to the size of their screen.

I also noticed that hardly anyone on the street or subway made eye contact. Yet only eye contact fully activates the parts of the brain that allow us to accurately perceive, process, and interact with others and our environment. When we make eye contact with another person, we literally *exchange our light with them*, which is why we can often sense someone looking at us *before we see them*. Even the brains of individuals who are legally blind get measurably activated when somebody looks at them.

But it is not just eye contact that allows us to see each other's light. Native Hawaiians traditionally acknowledge each other's divinity, or light, by sharing their breath. This ancient ritual, referred to as sharing *ha* (the breath of life), is done when welcoming a guest and is performed by both people pressing together the bridge of their noses while inhaling at the same time. In an age when human contact has, in many ways, been supplanted by wireless connections, and collaboration has been replaced by competition, we must never forget our universal need for connection with each other and the world we live in.

Aside from the ways that technology has impacted our vision, behavior, and inherent social skills, other adverse side effects are influencing our health and biological rhythms. One example is that smartphones, laptops, televisions, LED lamps, and many other devices employ a bright blue light that can confuse our brain into thinking that it is daytime, even during the night. The problem with exposure to this blue light at night is that its wavelengths impact our body's biological clock, suppressing the release of melatonin — the hormone that induces sleep — preventing us from falling asleep. The average person watching television or using a mobile device before bed may have difficulty falling and/or staying asleep, making early mornings particularly difficult.

New research also reveals that nighttime exposure to the same bright blue light emitted by our smartphones and computer screens can affect our metabolism, potentially causing us to gain weight and affect our body's ability to regulate glucose. Bright light exposure at night is associated with higher peak blood sugar levels. This is noteworthy because high blood sugar levels, over time, are associated with a higher risk for diabetes and can also lead to increased body fat and weight gain.

Given its detrimental effect on our metabolism and sleep-wake cycle, it is a good idea to turn off all blue-light screens and cover all blue LED lights at least two hours before bed. In addition, I suggest turning on the night shift function on your iPhone (or its equivalent on other phones). You can also download an app called f.lux (justgetflux.com) that adjusts the color of your computer's display to the time of day by reducing the blue light the screen emits. If using your computer and cell phone at night can significantly affect your body's metabolism and biological clock, what is the impact of keeping many of our cities lit up twenty-four hours a day?

Recent ground measurements and satellite data demonstrate that 83 percent of the world's population, and 99 percent of Europeans and people in the United States, live under skies at night that are nearly 10 percent brighter than their natural starry state. Individuals living in Singapore, Kuwait, and Qatar, for instance, experience the greatest amount of *light pollution* because they live under the brightest night skies, while those living in the Central African Republic and Madagascar are the least affected.

The night sky is so bright that according to Dr. Christopher Kyba at the German Research Centre for Geosciences, "Twenty percent of the people in Europe and 37 percent of the people in the US don't use their night vision." But aside from how light pollution is affecting our eyes, it is important to recognize its potential detrimental effects on our health.

Over the past decade, several studies have proposed that exposing ourselves to artificial light at night can increase the risk of cancer, especially those such as breast and prostate cancer that require hormones to grow. Aside from the fact that women who work night shifts have a higher incidence of breast cancer, a 2010 study conducted by Richard Stevens, an epidemiologist at the University of Connecticut, and colleagues at the University of Haifa indicates a 30 to 50 percent increased risk of breast cancer in countries with the greatest amount of light pollution versus those with the least amount.

But beyond its impact on vision, metabolism, sleep-wake cycles, and the development of certain cancers, light pollution may literally speed up the aging process. A recent study published in the journal *Current Biology* found that young mice exposed to artificial light around the clock suffer a range of health consequences typically associated with premature aging. Although we do not live under constant light for six months, as did the mice in this study, many of us who live in large cities are bombarded by light at night, even during sleep when our eyes are closed. In fact, up to 80 percent of the world's population lives under artificial light during the night.

To date, a variety of published studies have demonstrated that too much light at night disrupts our natural sleep cycles, contributing to health problems ranging from mood disorders, diabetes, and weight gain, to heart disease, cancer, and poor bone health. The good news, however, is that after the mice were returned to a normal light-dark cycle for two weeks, the inflammation, muscle weakness, and bone loss they experienced improved.

In an effort to provide cost and energy savings, many communities are now converting conventional streetlights to energy-efficient LEDs. Unfortunately, these high-intensity LEDs emit a significant amount of blue light, which impacts our sleep-wake cycle five times more than conventional streetlamps. In fact, recent large-scale surveys indicate that brighter residential nighttime lighting is associated with less sleep, poor sleep quality, more fatigue, obesity, and diminished daytime functioning.

Physicians at the 2016 annual meeting of the American Medical Association agree on the adverse effects of pervasive nighttime lighting and have developed specific guidelines for communities to minimize the detrimental human health and environmental effects of high-intensity LEDs.

To reduce the negative impact of light pollution on our health, researchers recommend that we consider the following suggestions:

1. Install room-darkening shades in bedrooms and, if possible, extend the dark period at night to nine or ten hours.
2. Avoid watching TV or working on the computer right before going to sleep. Turn off the lights, TV, and computer in the bedroom when you are sleeping, and if possible, turn off your wi-fi and avoid even brief light exposure at night.
3. If you typically get up at night to use the bathroom, install a dim red nightlight, as red light is less disturbing to our natural melatonin production than other wavelengths.

To preserve your eyes and optimize visual performance while reading, computing, or using your handheld device, please consider these suggestions:

1. Use ample lighting and, when possible, use natural light.
2. Face your desk toward a window.
3. Sit in a comfortable chair with your back erect.

4. Remember to breathe, blink, and look softly.
5. Hold your cell phone farther away from you, rather than closer to you.
6. Every fifteen minutes, look up, look away, breathe, and walk around for a minute.
7. Create a bookmark like the one below and use it when reading a book.

Today's technology is an amazing gift and has improved the quality of our lives in innumerable ways. However, just as it has many positive effects, technology also has many negative ones. But just like driving a car, we must stay awake and keep the car in the middle of the lane. We must remember how to be in the world and not of the world at the same time.

We have something that computers do not possess — an inseparable link to the animating force of this universe — and thus we have the ability to experience a level of intelligence that computers will never achieve.

An old proverb says, "If you can't beat them, join them." In the case of technology, I suggest doing neither. We can benefit from the technological developments of our time. However, we must not forget to take frequent breaks from what we are doing and, most importantly, take the time to look into each other's eyes, feel the light that connects us, and experience the essentialness of real human contact and communication. We need to allow our intuition to guide us as well as the information in our minds. And while computers may one day attain artificial intelligence status, they will never achieve the wisdom of that greater intelligence of life that directs us moment by moment.

CHAPTER THIRTEEN

Looking Less, Seeing More

My total conscious search in life has been for a new seeing, a new image, a new insight. This search not only includes the object, but the in-between place.

— LOUISE NEVELSON

One of the most common things I see these days is people multitasking, which often means that they are everywhere and nowhere at the same time. This is common in a technology-based society, as most people are so distracted or preoccupied that they are unable to focus their mind on what their eyes are seeing. Perhaps you have been in a conversation with someone and noticed that even though they are looking at you, they are obviously somewhere else. That is the most obvious sign that they are absent — their eyes are focused on one thing and their mind is focused on something else.

I first became aware of this in 1973, before the development and use of all our current technological innovations. I had just started my practice and noticed that almost every patient's history indicated that their eyes were weakening from year to year, and they were continually prescribed stronger and stronger lenses. Although these glasses improved their eyesight, they did not address the cause of the problem, so their eyes kept getting worse. Since I had had the same experience with my own eyes, I conducted a research study to determine a way to prescribe glasses that would improve a person's visual performance and prevent their eyesight from deteriorating further.

The results of that study, published in 1976, indicated that more than half of the participants were *looking too hard*. In addition, 69 percent of the subjects were not looking *where they thought they were looking*, signaling that their eyes and their mind were not converged on the same point. I started wondering whether there was a connection between this incongruity and the vision deterioration these individuals were experiencing.

Then I remembered that the father of behavioral optometry, Dr. A. M. Skeffington, proposed that the "socially compulsive, near-centered visual tasks" imposed by modern society are incompatible with our physiological makeup, triggering a stress response characterized by our eyes aiming closer than where they are focused. Since aiming and focusing involve both the eyes and the mind, you might say that Skeffington, in his own words, noticed a response to stress similar to the one I had found in my research study.

In his seminal work, *Vision: Its Development in Infant and Child*, child development expert Dr. Arnold Gesell also noted this incongruity between the eyes and the mind. Gesell described patients who looked at one spot with their eyes but elsewhere with their mind as being, "not 'spatially on' point of regard, though interpretively 'at' point of regard." Over the years I observed the very *incongruence* he described in thousands of patients — a result of excess visual effort fragmenting the fluidity of their perception and performance.

However, when I taught them the One-Minute Magic (Brock) String Exercise included in this chapter (see page 161), something startling happened. Once their visual and mental incongruence, or split-mindedness, was resolved, their presence and attention significantly improved as well as their performance in just about every other area of their lives. The results of that early study, along with my clinical experience, demonstrated that vision was designed to be effortless and supported my suspicion that, contrary to what I had learned, by looking less, we see more.

Are You Looking Where You Think You Are Looking?

Named after Dr. Frederick W. Brock, the Brock string is a commonly used tool in vision therapy. Use of the Brock string yielded such positive results that in the early 1980s I designed an electronic version for doctors to use with their patients. Inspired by the positive feedback from vision professionals, I developed a more advanced version in 2002. This vision training instrument became the first patented, FDA-cleared, and clinically proven medical device available to the public. A series of peer-reviewed studies showed significant improvement in overall vision performance, further confirming the wide-ranging benefits of reestablishing visual congruence. Those results are summarized below in four of our published studies.

In 2003 Pacific University College of Optometry revealed that using this device ten minutes a day, over a three-week period, yielded a significant increase in the ability to aim, track, focus, and use the eyes as a team. Reading efficiency and comprehension also improved. On quality of life questionnaires, subjects reported improved attention, alertness, and reading and athletic performance.

An independent study was completed in 2004 on the isolated effect of using this device on the batting performance of Little League baseball players. The results demonstrated a 90 percent improvement in batting performance after only three weeks of use. Shortly after the completion of the study, this team emerged from the loser's bracket to win their first league championship.

A third study was conducted in 2005 with the Maui County Police Department, whose members demonstrated significant improvement in visual attention, speed and span of recognition, and marksmanship. In addition, police recruit trainers noticed visible improvement in accuracy and appropriateness of physical response.

Following the same vision training protocol, a pilot study conducted in 2007 at Northeastern State University College of Optometry demonstrated significantly improved visual attention, focus, and depth perception in subjects previously diagnosed with ADHD. The improvements reported in these studies illustrate the far-reaching impact of vision training for optimizing the way we see and respond to the world.

When we look at something, we assume that we are looking directly at it. But how do we know for sure and what is the result of our eyes and mind not looking at the same place at the same time?

If, for instance, we are playing baseball and the pitcher throws us the ball, the degree to which we can accurately locate the ball in time and space determines if and when we will hit it. If our eyes and our mind are focused on the same place at the same time, we will be able to accurately perceive where the ball is (*congruence*) and when to swing at it (*coherence*), because the precision of our visual and mental alignment is reflected in the exactness of our physical movements.

Congruence and coherence, first discussed in chapter 2, refer to our seamless attunement with each moment, both individually and in relation to everything else. If, however, our eyes and our mind are not focused on the same place at the same time, it leads to *incongruence* and *incoherence* in our actions and a diminished capacity to perform. This may explain why certain individuals run habitually early or late — a misperception of how much time they have to reach their destination or how much distance they must cover in order to do so. This misalignment distorts our sense of time and space.

A few years ago I had the pleasure of working with a young golfer who demonstrated exceptional potential. When I observed her putting, I noticed that she was concentrating excessively, causing her eyes to overconverge. This affected her game because she perceived things to be closer than they actually were. However, once she became aware of this and incorporated vision training into her daily routine, her eyes and her mind merged and her game grew consistent, allowing her true talent to emerge. Today she is one of the top players in the Ladies Professional Golf Association. The ability to properly align our physical eyes with our mind's eye (or as Gesell put it, to be "'spatially on' point of regard") can unleash our potential not only as athletes but also as human beings.

My own vision problems started as a child, which left me with the impression that there was something wrong with me. Despite my insecurities I attended the University of Georgia and later earned doctorates in optometry and vision science. However, the reading demand was so hard on my eyes that I was given glasses within ten days of starting my undergraduate studies. Although I could see better with the glasses, the more I wore them, the worse my vision became — and reading remained a challenge. It seemed as if every six months or so I got a stronger prescription but still could not read for more than a few minutes without falling asleep.

The same pattern continued in optometry school, which made it so difficult to complete my assignments that by the end of my second year, I thought for sure I would fail. Then a miracle occurred. I was instructed to go to the clinic and have a vision exam. The student who examined me pointed out that my eyes were not aiming and teaming well and recommended that I do some vision training with a device he loaned me.

Sometime later I picked up the device and spent five minutes doing one of the prescribed exercises. I then proceeded to read for an hour at a level of comfort and comprehension I had never experienced in my life. It was as though a light turned on in my brain, triggering a facility that had been dormant to that point. I was so moved by what happened that I actually cried. I knew in that moment my life had changed.

I did the vision training exercises daily for two months and made the dean's list nearly every quarter until I graduated. That experience with vision training in 1971 allowed me to attend, read, and learn in ways I had not realized were possible, dissolving the belief that there was something wrong with me.

When my eyesight cleared in 1976, it not only altered my understanding of what it meant to see, but it also allowed my patients to recognize that such a possibility existed for them too. One young woman I worked with had worn glasses for seven years; she could not drive without them. Her story illustrates how knowledge is power.

After the economic crash in 2008, her family was forced to move from San Diego to Hawaii because they could no longer afford to keep their home, and Hawaii offered her father greater professional opportunity.

She was only twelve at the time, and was traumatized by leaving behind her home, school, and friends. Unable to cope with the situation, she fell into a slump of negativity and depression, and within six months noticed her eyesight failing.

When I asked her what happened to her eyesight, she said it was as if her fears were clouding her vision. She described feeling afraid of the world and withdrew from everyone and everything. When she finally came out of her shell and looked up, she could no longer see clearly. She was prescribed stronger glasses each year, which, according to her, became her security blanket.

During the initial visit I encouraged her to wear her glasses less and to do the Brock string exercise and the One-Minute Breath Meditation each day. After following my suggestions for a week, she shared the following:

> It's been both a struggle and a realization. Whenever I realize I can see, life seems to form itself for my eyes and I can make everything out. When I am having doubts, however, objects are blurrier. Since our visit, I'm also experiencing quite a roller coaster of emotions, stemming either from my temporary fears (as a low) or from my determination to grow (as a high).

My body feels like I have to get so much water out through my eyes by crying before my eyes can improve to the next level. Crazy as that may seem! My eyesight seems to become clearer after every episode of my crying. It feels like I'm seeing from my consciousness not my eyes, and every time my mind makes a leap in improvement, my eyes follow suit effortlessly.

Now It Is Your Turn

I will now share that possibility with you. First, let's see where your eyes and mind are focused when you are looking at something, and how that awareness can catalyze profound change.

When we look at something, we naturally assume that our eyes and mind are focused on the same point, as shown below. The line extending from each eye depicts where each eye is looking. The spoked circle represents the target being viewed, and the meeting point of the two lines represents where our eyes converge.

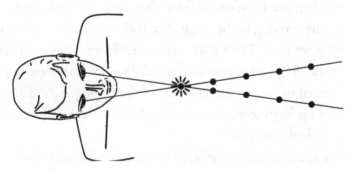

Eyes and mind congruently focused on the same point

In most cases, however, our eyes actually converge at a point closer or farther away than where we assume we are looking. The next illustration depicts a person whose eyes aim closer than the actual location of the object they are looking at. Even though they think they are looking at the object, their eyes are actually aiming at a point in front of it. While driving, they may react early because they think they are closer to the car in front of them than they actually are. Since time and distance are related, they may also have a tendency to arrive early for appointments because they think they have less time than they actually have.

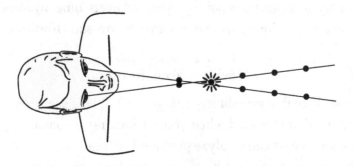

A person whose eyes aim closer than the actual location
of the object they are looking at

The next drawing represents a person whose eyes converge farther away than the location of the object they are looking at. They think they are looking at the target, but their eyes are actually aiming at a point beyond it. They may have a tendency to react at the last minute while driving because they think they are farther away from the car in front of them than they actually are. They may also tend to run late for appointments because they believe they have more time than they actually have.

Our judgments about time and space are based on where we think things are in relation to us. While driving, our response time is based on our estimate of the distance between us and the car in front of us. How far ahead we think it is determines how much time we think we have before we step on the brakes. Some people habitually run late because they think they have more time, while others run early because they do not think they have enough time. As you can see, there is more to vision than meets the eye.

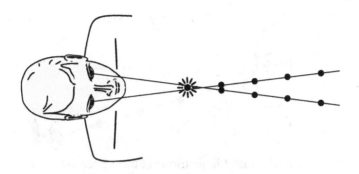

A person whose eyes aim farther away than the actual location
of the object they are looking at

THE ONE-MINUTE MAGIC (BROCK) STRING EXERCISE

To experience this yourself, you will need a piece of white
string about eight feet long and three or four large colored
beads approximately three-eighths of an inch in diameter.
Thread the string through the beads, tie a knot at each end of
the string, and then tie one end of the string to a doorknob, as
illustrated on the next page.

Position a chair about eight feet from the doorknob, so
when you are ready to sit down and begin the exercise, you
will be looking toward the doorknob, and the string will be
fully extended. Next, position each of the beads so they are
equally spaced between both ends of the string, making sure
that the bead closest to you is about twelve to sixteen inches
from your face. Sit down and hold one end of the string against
your upper lip or nose so that it is taut.

One-Minute Magic (Brock) String Exercise

Now look at the bead closest to the doorknob. If your two eyes are working together you should see the appearance of two strings pointing toward the bead you are looking at, forming a letter *V* (as illustrated below). If the bead you are looking at appears doubled, or if at times you see only one string, it may indicate that your two eyes are having difficulty working together or that one of your eyes stops working at times. If this does not improve after doing the exercise outlined in the next few pages, consider visiting a behavioral optometrist and possibly doing some vision training. If, however, you are seeing something similar to the illustration below, close one eye and then the other. You will notice that each time you close an eye, one of the strings disappears, indicating that each string is an imaginary frontal projection of one of your eyes.

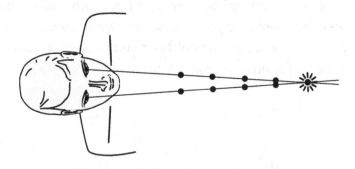

A person looking at a farther bead, whose eyes work together well and aim precisely at the actual location of the object they are looking at

Repeat this exercise while looking at one of the beads closest to you. If your two eyes are working together, you will once again see two strings aiming at the bead you are looking at. This time, however, the two strings will appear to intersect at or near the bead, forming a letter *X* as illustrated below.

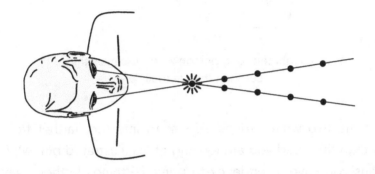

A person looking at a closer bead, whose eyes work together well and aim precisely at the actual location of the object they are looking at

Each time you look at the beads farther away, the strings will appear like a letter *V*. And each time you look at the beads closer to you, the strings will appear like a letter *X*. By creating the illusion of a string projecting out of each eye, this exercise allows you to "see" exactly where each eye is aiming when you are viewing something and whether your eyes are working together as a team.

Try this exercise again, looking at the bead closest to you, and notice where the two white strings are crossing in relation to the bead. If the two white strings appear to intersect closer to you than the bead that you are looking at (as illustrated below), it indicates that you have a tendency to perceive things closer than they actually are.

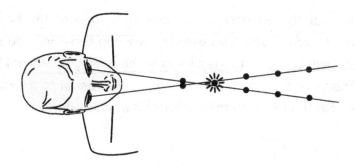

Visual alignment of a person who perceives things
closer than they actually are

If the two white strings appear to intersect farther from you than the bead you are looking at (as illustrated below), it means you have a tendency to perceive things farther away than they actually are.

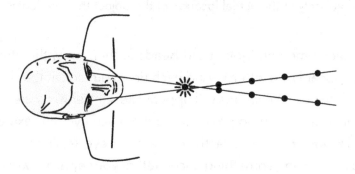

Visual alignment of a person who perceives things
farther away than they actually are

Now close your eyes for a second. Breathe, and when you feel ready, allow your eyes to naturally shift back and forth from the first bead that catches your attention to the next one that calls to you, and so on. As your eyes shift back and forth effortlessly, notice whether you see two strings that intersect like a letter *X* when you gaze at the beads up close and converge like a letter *V* when you view the beads farther away. Once you are able to do this exercise easily, gradually move the bead closest to you a bit closer, until it is about four to six inches away.

This awareness-expanding process can initially be done for one minute three times a day, eventually increasing to one minute each hour. As your eyes and mind merge, you will consistently notice the two white strings converging toward the bead you are looking at, and you will experience greater presence and attention than ever before.

Who's Noticing?

Now you have become aware of the fact that just because you think you are looking at something does not necessarily mean that your eyes are aiming directly at it. You have also been able to *see* where each of your eyes is aiming when you are gazing at something. But have you noticed who or what is noticing all this? Who is the "I" that notices where your physical eyes and mind are looking?

If we reflect on the changing nature of life, we see that everything comes and goes — from our thoughts and feelings, to the weather and the tides. Although our body, mind, and experiences change throughout our lifetime, the ever-present awareness witnessing these changes never vacillates — it is ageless and timeless.

We spend so much of our time trying to change the things in our life that are unacceptable to us, but liberation does not come from changing the outside world. It comes from realizing that we are the changeless eyes witnessing it. By aligning the physical eye, the mind's eye, and the eye of awareness, we reexperience our natural state of congruence and coherence with all that is — *oneness*.

CHAPTER FOURTEEN

What's Catching Your Eye?

Light created the eye as an organ with which to appreciate itself.
— GOETHE

As I discovered what it means to see and, most importantly, who is actually doing the seeing, I realized that vision training could do much more than just improve eyesight and visual performance — it can restore our congruency and coherence with the source of life itself. It can help us discover the true source of our seeing and the effortless guidance that it provides, allowing us to merge with the flow of life and experience our greatest potential. This state of fluidity is beautifully expressed in a passage from the fourth-century Chinese philosopher Zhuangzi:

> The baby looks at things all day without blinking;
> that is because his eyes are not focused on any particular object.
> He goes without knowing where he is going,
> and stops without knowing what he is doing.
> He merges himself within the surroundings
> and moves along with it.
> These are the principles of mental hygiene.

Zhuangzi describes the way in which a baby's eyes are seamlessly engaged in the movement of life. Although that fluidity is usually conditioned out of us and often forgotten as our mind develops, the innate desire for oneness is hardwired into the very fabric of the universe, always attracting us back to our source. That attractive force is the light that catches our eye, instigating the dynamic process of *aiming*, *focusing*, *tracking*, and *teaming*. Having explored these faculties in depth, I recognize them as fundamental to our ability to attend, assimilate, understand, and respond to life — in short, to fully experience *presence*.

As our eyes *aim*, initiating this process, they simultaneously *focus*, yielding clarity and thus an understanding of what has been seen. "I see" becomes synonymous with "I understand."

Since the landscape of life is constantly changing, our eyes continually *track* these changes, allowing us to dynamically aim and focus as needed at a given moment. This dynamic capacity to respond accurately and appropriately to what we perceive, which I elaborated on in chapter 13, illustrates how *coherence* is integral to every aspect of our development.

Concurrent with the eyes' process of aiming, focusing, and tracking, each eye has a slightly different view and interpretation of the world. Once these viewpoints are processed in the visual cortex and higher visual centers of the brain, we experience a single image in three dimensions. When two eyes merge their perspective, they are *teaming*, resulting in depth perception, which Dr. Arnold Gesell referred to as "the crown jewel of organic evolution."

Most of us limit our definition of depth perception to seeing the visible world stereoscopically, or three-dimensionally. When the eyes aim, focus, track, and team effectively, however, they establish a foundation that can afford us a depth of understanding beyond that which has been perceived by the physical eyes. This includes a glimpse of the *invisible world*, which exceeds the narrow 380–760 nanometer bandwidth of the electromagnetic spectrum, which, according to science, is the limit of human visual perception. We become aware of the roots of the tree, so to speak, as much as of the tree itself.

For most of us, vision has become *di-vision*, the process of splitting reality by choosing what we want over what we do not want. More than 1,400 years ago, Seng-Ts'an, the Third Zen Patriarch, wrote the following in his classic poem *Hsin-Hsin Ming*:

> The Great Way is not difficult for those who have no
>   preferences.
> When love and hate are both absent, everything becomes clear
>   and undisguised.
> Make the smallest distinction, however, and heaven and earth
>   are set infinitely apart.
> If you wish to see the truth, then hold no opinions for or against
>   anything.
> It is due to our choosing to accept or reject that we do not see
>   the true nature of things.

Ancient wisdom tells us that true vision is not binary but a state of undivided clarity and knowing, unobstructed by ideas and beliefs. Earlier in history Jesus says, "The light of the body is the eye; if, therefore, thine eye be single, thy whole body shall be full of light" (Matthew 6:22). This "singularity" of vision — and subsequent illumination — is a reflection of our innate ability to live in a state of oneness, fulfilling the ultimate potential of our visual process. By embodying the fluidity of Zhuangzi's baby, we do not have to work as hard as we think we do, since light naturally illuminates all that we are meant to see.

This is further confirmed by the fact that the retina of the eye is comprised of 95 percent rods and 5 percent cones, echoing the proportion of cognitive activities handled by the unconscious versus the conscious mind. Since the rods are designed for precognitive global viewing and the cones are intended for detailed local inspection, the eye, like the mind, confirms that we are meant to see without effort, physiologically mirroring the fluid line between *nondoing* and *doing*. But how do we allow that to happen when we have spent our whole life intentionally looking rather than instinctively seeing, even though our physiology is designed to respond to life rather than to initiate it?

In chapter 12 I discussed how most of us spend our days staring at our smartphones and computers, creating eyestrain and a constant compression of our visual field, often resulting in myopia. Even though this is presently an epidemic, the relationship between visual confinement and myopia is not new.

The early work of researcher Dr. Francis Young demonstrated that when monkeys are placed in a visually confined environment, approximately 75 percent become myopic within a three-month period. Furthermore, Navy submarine personnel, working in a confined visual environment, develop myopia much faster than other military personnel. Yet in another study conducted on indigenous cultures that did not read or engage in close-up work, Young recorded virtually no incidence of myopia.

As a result of confining our vision for prolonged periods, we diminish our eyes' capacity to dynamically shift between close-up and wider-focused visual demands. Since the eyes are frontal extensions of the brain, informing our body how to move and respond to life, maintaining visual flexibility is critical to everything we do. Thus, the weakening of this visual agility compromises our ability to function with congruence, coherence, and fluidity, reducing our ability to quickly, accurately, and efficiently respond to the ever-changing landscape of life. Taken a step further, Dr. Gesell writes, "If the eye should become excessively specialized, it might too soon spell doom for the species."

Although Gesell expressed his concern in 1949, there could not be a more important time in history to discuss this prospect. Because our eyes guide every move we make and how we see the world, they also determine how we respond to it. On a deeper level, I think Gesell was forewarning us about the dire consequences of losing our vision, both literally and figuratively.

Although many people think vision training is just eye exercises, it is really an awareness-expanding process about seeing without effort — *by heart* rather than through the mind and the accumulated beliefs that limit our perception. We cannot return to the purity of vision of Zhuangzi's baby if we are always *looking for life* instead of letting *life look for us*. The guidance that life provides us through light itself accompanies us in every moment of our lives.

The Experiment

In the introduction I mentioned a one-week experiment I did many years ago when my children were very young. It was based on the idea that anything that caught my eye was looking for me. For a week, anything that entered my awareness became my responsibility, anything that was my responsibility I would attend to, and anything I attended to I would complete. The impact of that experiment was so powerful that it became the cornerstone of my life, showing me how following life's guidance takes us from one moment to another, creating a life filled with purpose and meaning.

So how can we automatically respond to what's catching our eye? First we must recognize that light is catching our eye — the same light the Bible refers to as God and physicists describe as the foundation of all that is. This light creates, guides, and nourishes the development and evolvement of all living things. This same light directs a seed to grow into a tree that bears fruit, feeds the world, and then populates the earth with more seeds.

Once we recognize this truth, we respond to whatever calls us.

We need not prioritize anything, because the intelligence of life has already done that for us. And everything in life has equal value. The way you wash your dishes is no different than the way you wash your infant's back. So if a bill comes in the mail, pay it. When the phone rings, answer it. When you are inspired, create. When you feel love, express it. When a problem lands in your lap, welcome it and then deal with it. Embrace life and it will guide you toward optimal health and well-being — not only yours but also the health and well-being of those around you. Your life, as Gandhi once said, is your message, and your message is contagious. Responding to what catches your eye not only sets you free, it sets everyone free.

We often speak about living in the moment or wanting to be "spiritual," but being spiritual is not about being anything but rather taking care of what is in front of you, recognizing that your life is your meditation. *With clarity we become ordinary* — simply taking care of whatever comes before us. Following this process, we develop a knowing that whatever shows up, we will meet.

In the past, when I did not take care of things in the moment, they got backed up and I felt overwhelmed. Then I discovered that life never brings us anything at the wrong time. Everything in nature works so simply and beautifully.

So Let's Begin

For the next twenty-four hours, respond to whatever enters your awareness. Everything you notice is looking for you, so take care of it and complete it. If you notice your bed needs to be made, make it. If a dish is in the sink, even if it is not yours, wash it, dry it, and put it away. If you owe someone money or receive a bill that you are unable to pay, call them well in advance (not at the last minute), and let them know the circumstances and assure them that you will take care of it as soon as possible. Show your love and appreciation when you feel it, by saying "thank you" and "I love you" to those around you. Clean your surroundings as soon as you notice something needs tending to. When something needs repair, attend to it without putting it off. Return emails and phone calls in a reasonable period of time. When someone needs help, help them. Wipe off the toilet seat, dry the area next to the sink, take out the trash, and express your appreciation when someone has helped you or made a meal for you. In essence, stop pretending you do not see and start acknowledging how much you do see.

By recognizing and accepting how much we see, we ignite a process that continuously expands consciousness. Simply attending to whatever enters our awareness is the most valuable practice we have for self-development. Our real insights come from the everyday experience of *presence* — in our personal relationships, the way we run our businesses, and in honoring our commitments. In opening our eyes to everything that touches us, we practice the highest level of vision.

Planting Seeds of Goodness

I once heard a story about an old rabbi on his deathbed who was sharing about his lifelong attempt to change the world. He said that as a young man, he traveled from country to country, sharing his message, but nothing happened. So he decided to spread his teachings within his own country. Once again, nothing happened. So he focused his efforts on his own community. To his amazement, no one would listen. Eventually he went home, a bit dejected, and began speaking with his own wife and children. But even they were too busy to listen. So he paused for a moment, and after a deep sigh he said, *If only I would have started with myself.*

When we try to contemplate huge change, such as saving the Amazon rain forest or ending world hunger, we forget that change begins with us. As we awaken to the fact that light is animating and guiding us, we realize that taking care of what is in front of us — simply expressing our gratitude, listening to someone's story, or cheering someone up with a smile or a warm embrace — profoundly impacts the world. Like Johnny Appleseed, we plant seeds of goodness wherever we go.

EPILOGUE

Our purpose is hidden in our joy, our inspiration, our excitement. As we act on what shows up in our life, our purpose shows up.

— James King

The essential message of this book is that your life is looking for you, continually guiding you through the process of presence so that you may fulfill your reason for being. This fundamental fact is not only true for humans but also for everything that exists. We are being guided — not occasionally — always! The key to our awakening, freedom, contentment, and highest potential is all the same. Do what you love, love what you do, and the world will come to you. This is because doing what you love is the same as following your guidance, creating a foundation of authentic trust, unconditional love, absolute integrity, and unquestionable respect for the wisdom of life and your own sense of knowing.

Throughout the preceding chapters I shared experiences that have awoken me to a new reality. The question is how does *seeing* in this new way affect our everyday life. From my experience, everything looks the same and yet it is totally different. I have a continuously expanding acceptance for life just as it is, a realization that life includes many experiences, some pleasant and some not so pleasant.

I have also awakened to the fact that, while none of us feel comfortable with pain, loss, illness, financial worry, or relational stress, these experiences are all an integral part of our life's journey and foundational to our spiritual development.

I did not read much as a child, so most of what I learned did not come from my formal education but from my direct experience. In the process I discovered my inclusive nature and realized that life is not about them versus me. It is always about "us" — all of us. Inclusivity grows out of the humility gained by realizing that we each have a job to do, and that job is essential to the integrity of the whole, inseparably linking us to everything else.

When I am involved in something, I am focused on every detail. That focus comes from living choicelessly because when we are guided by life there are no choices, decisions, or options to consider. All our energy is naturally focused on the guidance we have received, because we know that everything we are directed to accomplish is a sacred task. Something keeps us on track and keeps us going no matter what happens in our life.

Our physical eyes are designed to see the outer world of form. Our spiritual eyes are designed to see the invisible. When these eyes collaborate fluidly, congruence and coherence meld into one and signal the beginning of a new way of seeing and being. That is *presence*.

With presence, we respond to life like the leaves of a sun-loving plant turning toward the essence of the universe — *light*. This essence is the invisible force that illuminates all that is visible — a field of awareness that sees when our physical eyes are closed and watches our dreams while we sleep.

Throughout this book I have attempted to support my insights with scientific evidence. However, it is important to realize that while we must recognize the great achievements of modern science, we must also realize that science cannot provide us an explanation about what is truly essential to the human spirit.

In *Nature and the Greeks*, Austrian physicist and Nobel laureate Erwin Schrödinger writes:

> The scientific picture of the real world around me is very deficient. It gives a lot of factual information, puts all our experience in a magnificently consistent order, but it is ghastly silent about all and sundry that is really near to our heart, that really matters to us. It cannot tell us a word about red and blue, bitter and sweet, physical pain and physical delight; it knows nothing of beautiful and ugly, good or bad, God and eternity. Science sometimes pretends to answer questions in these domains, but the answers are very often so silly that we are not inclined to take them seriously.

Now that I am seventy, my youthful search for scientific truth has been replaced by a *sense of knowing* that requires no substantiation but rather a surrendering to my *not knowing*, which allows true wisdom to reveal itself. I feel humbled whenever such whispers traverse my awareness, blessing me with an opportunity not only to grow but also to support others on their journey.

At this point I feel that our hindsight, insight, and foresight combine to create *our total vision*, dissolving our *di-vision* and opening our eyes to the divinity in others and ourselves. While working as an optometrist, vision scientist, and syntonic practitioner were invaluable to the distillation of my *own* vision, I find it mysteriously fascinating how the intelligence of life initially inspired me to look deeply into these areas of science as a means of preparing me for my life's work, and ultimately forced me to let go of these modalities so that my *presence* finally emerged — and thus, my purpose.

Today, my greatest pleasure is in holding the hands of a group of individuals whom I mentor. This work is based on three principles:

1. Healing relationships cannot be hierarchical — everyone involved must be the same "height" or equally accessible.
2. Nothing is wrong with us and therefore nothing requires

fixing. In my experience, spending time with another who sees us as whole is often enough to transform the way in which we see ourselves. In this way, *contact is content*.

3. Mentorship is about preparing an individual for the most important day of their lives, the day they spread their wings and leave the nest, soaring through the landscape of their life in a return to their essence.

As our essence grows more visible in our walk, our talk, the way we listen, how we handle our daily affairs, and show up for each other, our vision truly reaches and touches the world, for we are the light that has always guided and illuminated our journey.

ACKNOWLEDGMENTS

Many individuals contributed to this book. Some inspired me, others helped me see more clearly, and some worked with me to build this book one page at a time. Each contribution distilled the essence that I had hoped to communicate in words.

First, I want to thank my parents, Sonia and Joseph Liberman, for they are the source of truth and integrity that allows me to walk upright in this world.

Trying to express what one knows by heart is not an easy task. However, I was blessed to have the support of three extraordinary writers. First, my son, Erik, helped me create the original version of this book, titled *Depth Perception*. Then, John Nelson assisted me in transforming and expanding the original memoir into a broader, more rooted message. Finally, my daughter, Gina, helped me clarify and fine-tune the book's message into what you have just read.

In addition, I want to thank my dear friends Dr. Brian Breiling, Dr. Jennifer Nelson, and David (Ilili) Kapralik. I also want to acknowledge Heidi Erhardt, Stephanie Tade, and Michael Ebeling for their encouragement, contributions, and loving support; Lauren Harris (www.teawaterdesigns.com) for her beautiful illustrations; and Peter Straubinger for permission to use the information and research contained in his wonderful documentary, *In the Beginning There Was Light*.

A special thanks to my agent, Steve Harris, and to Georgia Hughes, Marc Allen, and the entire New World Library publishing team for believing in me and the message of this book, and for bringing this project to fruition.

And finally, I am deeply appreciative of my partner, Deborah, for her love and ongoing support during the writing of this book.

NOTES

Epigraph

Page vii, *"My brain is only a receiver..."*: Nikola Tesla, in Nikola Tesla and David H. Childress, *The Fantastic Inventions of Nikola Tesla* (Stelle, IL: Adventures Unlimited Press, 1993), 1.

Chapter One: How Light Guides Us

Page 11, *Some researchers believe that birds*: Ed Yong, "Humans Have a Magnetic Sensor in Our Eyes, but Can We Detect Magnetic Fields?" *Discover*, June 21, 2011, http://blogs.discovermagazine.com/notrocketscience /2011/06/21/humans-have-a-magnetic-sensor-in-our-eyes-but-can-we-see -magnetic-fields/#.VwtLtquBDCx.

Page 12, *we too may be equipped with such a sixth sense*: Lauren E. Foley, Robert J. Gegear, and Steven M. Reppert, "Human Cryptochrome Exhibits Light-Dependent Magnetosensitivity," *Nature Communications* 2 (2011), doi:10.1038 /ncomms1364.

Page 13, *"I have always considered myself unable to understand..."*: Dan Hofstadter, *The Earth Moves: Galileo and the Roman Inquisition* (New York: W. W. Norton, 2010), 68.

Page 13, *"For the rest of my life I will reflect on what light is!"*: Albert Einstein, in William W. Hay, *Experimenting on a Small Planet: A History of Scientific Discoveries, a Future of Climate Change and Global Warming* (New York: Springer Nature, 2016), 185.

Page 13, *for light beams, time and space do not exist*: Peter Russell, "From Science to God: The Journey of a Devout Skeptic," *Bridges Magazine* 1 (2009): 8–11, http://issseem.org/content/uploads/files/Bridges_2009_1.pdf.

Page 14, *"Light is energy and it's also information…"*: David Bohm, *The Essential David Bohm*, ed. Lee Nichol (Abingdon-on-Thames, UK: Routledge, 2003), 154.

Page 14, *"a sensation of feeling light waves through our eyes…"*: Walter Russell, *The Secret of Light* (Waynesboro, VA: University of Science and Philosophy, 1947), 43, 44.

Page 14, *David Bohm took things a step further*: David Bohm, "Of Matter and Meaning: The Super-Implicate Order," *Re Vision* 6, no. 1 (Spring 1983): 34–44.

Page 15, *"Are not gross bodies and light convertible…"*: Isaac Newton, *Opticks: Or, A Treatise of the Reflections, Refractions, Inflections and Colours of Light*, 2nd ed. (London: Sam Smith and Ben, Walford, 1717), 349.

Page 17, *the human eye can detect a single photon of light*: Jonathan N. Tinsley, Maxim I. Molodtsov, Robert Prevedel, David Wartmann, Jofre Espigulé-Pons, Mattias Lauwers, and Alipasha Vaziri, "Direct Detection of a Single Photon by Humans," *Nature Communications* 7 (2016), doi:10.1038/ncomms 12172.

Page 17, *"The most amazing thing…"*: Alipasha Vaziri, cited in Mary Pascaline, "Human Eye Can Detect Even Individual Photons, the Smallest Unit of Light: Study," *International Business Times*, July 21, 2016, http://www.ibtimes.com/human-eye-can-detect-even-individual-photons-smallest-unit-light-study-2393524.

Page 17, *The process of vision*: "Discovery by SU Physicist Alters Conventional Understanding of Sight," *Syracuse University News*, June 24, 2011, http://www.syr.edu/news/articles/2011/as-sight-research-06-11.html.

Page 19, *the order of endocrine entrainment in the human body*: Leonard A. Wisneski, "A Unified Energy Field Theory of Physiology and Healing," *Stress Medicine* 13, no. 4 (1997): 259–65.

Page 19, *light also guides the trillions of cells in our body*: Tiina Karu, "Mitochondrial Mechanisms of Photobiomodulation," YouTube, November 22, 2014, https://www.youtube.com/watch?v=NIU2oLbe4-I (presentation given at the 2011 conference of the International Light Association in Ste-Adèle, Canada).

Page 19, *This is the energy used by cells*: Ralph Hill, "Photomodulation with LED Light Sources," *beautymag online*, http://beautymagonline.com/technology-treatments/20-technology-treatments/1159-photo modulation-2.

Page 19, *"All the energy which we take into our bodies…"*: Albert Szent-Gyorgyi, *Introduction to a Submolecular Biology* (New York: Academic Press, 1960).

Chapter Two: The Light within Us

Page 22, *a lag exists between seeing something*: Michael H. Herzog, Thomas Kammer, Frank Scharnowski, "Time Slices: What Is the Duration of a Percept?" *PLOS Biology* 14, no. 6 (2016), doi.org/10.1371/journal.pbio.1002493.

Page 26, *"The pupils cannot lie…"*: Desmond Morris, *The Human Animal: A Personal View of the Human Species* (New York: Crown, 1994), 130.

Page 26, *"early stages of courtship the eyes transmit vital signals…"*: Morris, *The Human Animal*, 130.

Page 27, *when we are deeply involved in speaking*: Olivia Kang and Thalia Wheatley, "Pupil Dilation Patterns Spontaneously Synchronize across Individuals during Shared Attention," *Journal of Experimental Psychology: General* 146, no. 4 (2017): 569–76.

Page 28, *"we use only one-seventh of our lungs…"*: Swami Satchidananda, *Pathways to Peace* (Buckingham, VA: Integral Yoga Publications, 2004), 1.

Page 33, *experienced meditators who claim to be aware during deep sleep*: Fabio Ferrarelli et al., "Experienced Mindfulness Meditators Exhibit Higher Parietal-Occipital EEG Gamma Activity during NREM Sleep," *PLOS ONE* 8, no. 8 (2013), doi.org/10.1371/journal.pone.0073417.

Page 33, *consciousness does not turn off*: Jennifer M. Windt, Tore Nielsen, and Evan Thompson, "Does Consciousness Disappear in Dreamless Sleep?" *Trends in Cognitive Sciences* 20, no. 12 (December 2016): 871–82, http://dx.doi.org/10.1016/j.tics.2016.09.006.

Page 33, *"Consciousness, in the sense of sheer awareness or feeling of being or existing…"*: Evan Thompson, cited in Olivia Goldhill, "Cognitive Science Backs Up the Ancient Indian Philosophy That We're Conscious Even in Deep Sleep," *Quartz India*, December 4, 2016, http://qz.com/852486

/cognitive-science-backs-up-the-ancient-indian-philosophy-that-were
-conscious-even-in-deep-sleep.

Chapter Three: Living on Light

Page 35, *In 1896 Wilbur Atwater and Francis Benedict*: "The Calorie Myth," *In the Beginning There Was Light*, http://www.lightdocumentary.com /the-calorie-myth.html.

Page 35, *a significant discrepancy between the theoretical amounts of energy*: P. Webb, J. F. Annis, and S. J. Troutman Jr., "Energy Balance in Man Measured by Direct and Indirect Calorimetry," *American Journal of Clinical Nutrition* 33, no. 6 (June 1980): 1287–98, http://ajcn.nutrition.org /content/33/6/1287.abstract.

Page 36, *the case of yogi Prahlad Jani*: Tom Rawstorne, "The Man Who Says He Hasn't Eaten of Drunk for 70 Years: Why Are Eminent Doctors Taking Him Seriously?" *Daily Mail*, last modified May 7, 2010, http://www.daily mail.co.uk/news/article-1274779/The-man-says-eaten-drunk-70-years -Why-eminent-doctors-taking-seriously.html.

Page 36, *In 2003 Prahlad Jani first underwent*: Rajeev Khanna, "Fasting Fakir Flummoxes Physicians," BBC News, last modified November 25, 2003, http://news.bbc.co.uk/2/hi/south_asia/3236118.stm.

Page 37, *"We are all scientifically educated…"*: Sudhir Shah, cited in "The Case of Prahlad Jani," *In the Beginning There Was Light*, http://www.light documentary.com/prahlad-jani.html, accessed September 15, 2017.

Page 37, *In 2010 Jani was once again rigorously evaluated*: Sanal Edamaruku, "India's Man Who Lives on Sunshine," *Guardian*, last modified May 18, 2010, http://www.theguardian.com/commentisfree/belief/2010/may/18 /prahlad-jani-india-sunshine.

Page 37, *After fifteen days of not eating*: "Experts Baffled as Mataji's Medical Reports Are Normal," *DNA India*, last modified May 7, 2010, http://www .dnaindia.com/india/report-experts-baffled-as-mataji-s-medical-reports -are-normal-1380169.

Page 37, *Jani was in better health*: Rawstorne, "The Man Who Says He Hasn't Eaten or Drunk for 70 Years."

Page 37, *further studies were planned to investigate*: "Study Proves Gujarat Man's Claim of Living without Food, Water," *DNA India*, last modified July 17, 2010, http://www.dnaindia.com/india/report-study-proves-gujarat-man-s -claim-of-living-without-food-water-1411144.

Page 37, *"Why should a living being not be able…"*: Nikola Tesla, "Talking with the Planets," *Collier's Weekly*, February 9, 1901, http://teslacollection.com /tesla_articles/1901/colliers/nikola_tesla/talking_with_the_planets.

Page 38, *"Experimental evidence shows that light imparts…"*: Gerald Pollack, in "How 'Breatharianism' Works: The Science of Light and Water," *Light Documentary* (blog), March 18, 2016, https://lightdocumentary.space /2016/03/18/how-breatharianism-works-the-science-of-light-and-water.

Page 38, *Fourth-phase water, H_3O_2, is more viscous*: Gerald Pollack, "Can Humans Harvest the Sun's Energy Directly Like Plants?" GreenMedInfo .com, last modified June 1, 2015, http://www.greenmedinfo.com/blog /can-humans-photosynthesize-1.

Page 38, *the powerful documentary by P. A. Straubinger*: P. A. Straubinger, *In the Beginning There was Light* (Austria, 2010) DVD; http://www.light documentary.com.

Page 39, *only one-third of the energy produced by our body*: Alexander Wunsch, cited in Joseph Mercola, "How LED Lighting May Compromise Your Health," Mercola.com, last modified October 23, 2016, http://articles .mercola.com/sites/articles/archive/2016/10/23/near-infrared-led -lighting.aspx?utm_source=dnl&utm_medium=email&utm_content=art 1&utm_campaign=20161023Z1&et_cid=DM123594&et_rid=1723202311.

Page 39, *It can help us recover from illness and injury*: Kay Uzoma, "The Benefits of a Three-Day Juice Fast," Livestrong.com, last modified November 2, 2015, http://www.livestrong.com/article/422825-benefits-of-fasting -for-the-immune-system.

Page 40, *underfed lab animals live longer, healthier lives*: Annie Sneed, "Hunger Gains: A New Idea of Why Eating Less Increases Life Span," *Scientific American*, last modified April 14, 2015, http://www.scientificamerican .com/article/hunger-gains-a-new-idea-of-why-eating-less-increases-life -span.

Page 40, *"cutting back on food leads to increased rates…"*: Margo Adler, cited in Jo Willey, "Eat Less, Live Longer: Cutting Back on Food Can Help Repair the Body, Says New Study," *Express*, last modified March 19, 2014, http://www.express.co.uk/life-style/health/465647/Eat-less-live-longer -Cutting-back-on-food-can-help-repair-the-body-says-new-study.

Page 40, *The significance of this is paramount, as vitamin D deficiency*: Jordan Lite, "Vitamin D Deficiency Soars in the U.S., Study Says," *Scientific*

American, last modified March 23, 2009, http://www.scientificamerican
.com/article/vitamin-d-deficiency-united-states.

Page 40, *strongly linked to a rise in the incidence of the "diseases of civilization"*:
Stefan Silbernagl et al., *Taschenatlas der Physiologie* (Stuttgart, Germany:
Thieme, 2001).

Page 40, *Scientists have also confirmed a significant relationship*: University of Ex-
eter, "Link between Vitamin D, Dementia Risk Confirmed," *ScienceDaily*,
August 6, 2014, http://www.sciencedaily.com/releases/2014/08/1408061
61659.htm.

Page 41, *"You are responsible for a spontaneous remission of poor vision…"*: Mary
G., letter to author, March 30, 1998.

Page 41, *"I remember being excited about going to the doctor's office…"*:
Natalie G., email to author, September 10, 2013.

Chapter Four: The Intelligence of Life

Page 44, *"The entire cosmos is organized by an ordering force…"*: Marcus
Aurelius, *The Essential Marcus Aurelius*, trans. Jacob Needleman and John
P. Piazza (New York: Tarcher, 2008), xxv.

Page 44, *"There is a force in the universe…"*: Mahatma Gandhi, in David L.
Kahn, *Boundless Paradox: Awakening in the Collective Dream* (Morrisville,
NC: lulu.com, 2015), Kindle.

Page 47, *all living organisms, including humans*: Marco Bischof, "Biophotons:
The Light in Our Cells," *Journal of Optometric Phototherapy* (March 2005):
1–5; and "What Is Biophoton Science?" Health Angel Foundation, http://
www.biontology.com/research/what-is-biophoton-science.

Page 47, *more than half of all marine organisms*: Anne Bolen, "Living Light:
Glowing Organisms Have Captured Our Curiosity for Centuries, yet
Scientists Are Still Discovering How They Glow — and Why," *National
Wildlife*, May 25, 2016, https://www.nwf.org/Magazines/National
-Wildlife/2016/JuneJuly/Animals/Bioluminescence; and Rachel Nuwer,
"Way More Fish Can Make Their Own Light Than We Thought," Smith-
sonian.com, June 8, 2016, http://www.smithsonianmag.com/science
-nature/way-more-fish-can-make-their-own-light-we-thought-1809
59346/?no-ist.

Page 47, *certain creatures absorb light and then reemit it as a different color*: Russ
Swan, "Glow in the SHARK: Marine Creatures Radiate More Light the

Deeper They Swim and May Use the Trick to 'Talk' to Each Other," *Daily Mail*, last modified April 26, 2016, http://www.dailymail.co.uk/science tech/article-3559484/Glow-SHARK-Marine-creatures-radiate-light -deeper-swim-use-trick-talk-other.html.

Page 48, *the human body consists of approximately thirty-seven trillion cells*: Eva Bianconi et al., "An Estimation of the Number of Cells in the Human Body," *Annals of Human Biology* 40, no. 6 (2013), http://dx.doi.org /10.3109/03014460.2013.807878.

Page 48, *a cell's ability to literally "see"*: Guenter Albrecht-Buehler, "Cell Intelligence," last updated April 9, 2013, http://www.basic.northwestern .edu/g-buehler/frame.htm.

Page 48, *But new research, published in the journal* Science: Kanupriya Pande et al., "Femtosecond Structural Dynamics Drives the Trans/Cis Isomerization in Photoactive Yellow Protein," *Science* 352, no. 6286 (May 6, 2016): 725–29, doi:10.1126/science.aad5081.

Page 49, *"Everything is connected to everything else…"*: David Bohm, in John Gribbin, *Schrodinger's Kittens and the Search for Reality: Solving the Quantum Mysteries* (New York: Back Bay Books, 1996), 159.

Page 49, *"trees in the forest [as] social beings…"*: Sally McGrane, "German Forest Ranger Finds That Trees Have Social Networks, Too," *New York Times*, January 29, 2016, https://www.nytimes.com/2016/01/30/world /europe/german-forest-ranger-finds-that-trees-have-social-networks-too .html; and Peter Wohlleben, *The Hidden Life of Trees: What They Feel, How They Communicate: Discoveries from a Secret World* (Vancouver, BC: Greystone Books, 2016).

Page 49, *When we are feeling love, intimacy, gratitude, or appreciation*: Arjun Walia, "Not Just Brain to Body: Researchers Discover That the Heart Sends Signals to the Brain," *Collective Evolution*, October 30, 2015, http://www.collective-evolution.com/2015/10/30/not-just-brain-to -body-researchers-discover-that-the-heart-sends-signals-to-the-brain.

Page 50, *"I am not aware of any other factor in medicine…"*: Dean Ornish, *Love and Survival: The Scientific Basis for the Healing Power of Intimacy* (New York: HarperCollins, 1998), chap. 1.

Page 53, *"If we leave nature alone…"*: Molière, *The Dramatic Works of Molière, Volume 3*, ed. Henry Van Laun (Philadelphia: Gebbie & Barrie Publishers, 1879), 548.

Page 55, *"Miracles occur naturally as expressions of love…"*: Helen Schucman, *A*

Course in Miracles, combined volume, 3rd ed. (Mill Valley, CA: Foundation for Inner Peace, 2007), 3.

Chapter Five: The Light in Our Dreams

Page 57, *"One views a region of space filled with light…"*: Arthur Zajonc, *Catching the Light: The Entwined History of Light and Mind* (New York: Oxford University Press, 1993), 2.

Page 58, *"absolute darkness!…"*: Zajonc, *Catching the Light*, 2.

Page 59, *"I regard consciousness as fundamental…"*: *The Observer*, January 25, 1931, as cited in "Max Planck," Wikiquote, last modified August 5, 2017, https://en.wikiquote.org/wiki/Max_Planck.

Page 59, *"For every inside there is an outside…"*: Alan Watts, *Man, Nature, and the Nature of Man* (New York: Macmillan Audio, 1991), audiobook.

Page 60, *"Consciousness is the ground of being that conceives…"*: Deepak Chopra, "Explorations in Consciousness and Healing," *Bridges Magazine* 20, no. 1 (2010): 4.

Page 60, *"The cosmos is within us…"*: Carl Sagan, in Karen Schroeder Sorensen, *Cosmos and the Rhetoric of Popular Science* (Maryland: Lexington Books, 2017), 51.

Page 63, *"The interpretation of dreams is the royal road…"*: Sigmund Freud, cited in Jonathan Lear, *Freud*, 2nd ed. (New York: Routledge, 2015), 90.

Chapter Six: Escaping the Mind Field

Page 66, *"The widespread and pervasive distinctions between people…"*: David Bohm, *Wholeness and the Implicate Order* (London: Routledge & Kegan Paul, 1980), xii.

Page 66, *the entire universe is comprised of a singular*: Deepak Chopra, "Explorations in Consciousness" (keynote address, at ISSSEEM annual conference, Westminster, CO, June 28, 2009); and Mark Comings, "The Quantum Plenum: The Hidden Key to Life, Energetics and Sentience," *Bridges Magazine* 17, no. 1 (Spring 2006): 4–13, 20.

Page 66, *ancient mystical texts have historically referred to God*: Peter Russell, *From Science to God: A Physicist's Journey into the Mystery of Consciousness* (Novato, CA: New World Library, 2004), chap. 6.

Page 66, *We cannot detach ourselves*: "Observer Effect," Wikipedia, last modified September 25, 2017, https://simple.wikipedia.org/wiki/Observer_effect.

Page 67, *"If the conscious mind is like a general..."*: David Brooks, *The Social Animal: The Hidden Sources of Love, Character, and Achievement* (New York: Random House, 2011), ix.

Page 68, *"The conscious self is unconscious of most things..."*: Amit Goswami, personal conversation with author, February 2014.

Page 70, *"We shall not cease from exploration..."*: T. S. Eliot, "Little Gidding," *Four Quartets* (New York: Faber and Faber, 1942), 144–45.

Page 72, *when Tibetan Buddhists were meditating*: Andrew Newberg, Eugene D'Aquili, and Vince Rause, *Why God Won't Go Away: Brain Science and the Biology of Belief* (New York: Ballantine Books, 2002).

Page 72, *a considerable increase in activity in the brain area*: Jon Kabat-Zinn and Richard J. Davidson, *The Mind's Own Physician: A Scientific Dialogue with the Dalai Lama on the Healing Power of Meditation* (Oakland, CA: New Harbinger, 2013).

Page 73, *biophoton emission in healthy transcendental meditation practitioners*: Roeland Van Wijk, Guido Godaert, and Eduard P. A. Van Wijk, "Human Ultra Weak Light Emission in Consciousness Research," in Jason T. Locks, ed., *New Research on Consciousness* (Hauppauge, NY: Nova Science, 2006).

Page 73, *the body functions more harmoniously*: Roeland Van Wijk, *Light in Shaping Life: Biophotons in Biology and Medicine* (Amersfoort, Netherlands: Meluna Research, 2014).

Page 74, *"When you make the two one..."*: Saying 22, *The Gospel of Thomas*, trans. Thomas O. Lambdin, Gnostic Society Library, http://gnosis.org/naghamm/gthlamb.html, accessed September 20, 2017.

Page 74, *"If the doors of perception were cleansed..."*: Steve Clark and Jason Whittaker, eds. *Blake, Modernity and Popular Culture* (Basingstoke, UK: Palgrave Macmillan, 2007), 177.

Page 74, *"Thoughts arise because of the thinker..."*: Ramana Maharshi, *The Essential Teachings of Ramana Maharshi: A Visual Journey*, ed. Matthew Greenblatt (Carlsbad, CA: Inner Directions, 2001), 15.

Chapter Seven: Discovering the Genius within Us

Page 77, *"divine influence directly and immediately exerted..."*: "Inspiration," Dictionary.com, http://www.dictionary.com/browse/inspiration?s=ts.

Page 77, *only 5 percent of our cognitive activities*: Marc Van Rymenant, "95

Percent of Brain Activity Is Beyond Our Conscious Awareness," *Simplifying Interfaces* (blog), August 1, 2008, http://www.simplifyinginterfaces.com/2008/08/01/95-percent-of-brain-activity-is-beyond-our-conscious-awareness.

Page 77, *"Some researchers have gone so far…"*: Timothy D. Wilson, *Strangers to Ourselves: Discovering the Adaptive Unconscious* (Cambridge, MA: Belknap Press, 2002), 24.

Page 78, *The human brain has two very different processing systems*: Jag Bhalla, "Kahneman's Mind-Clarifying Strangers: System 1 & System 2," Big Think, http://bigthink.com/errors-we-live-by/kahnemans-mind-clarifying-biases, accessed September 20, 2016.

Page 78, *Intuition is part of the first system*: Antoine Bechara et al., "Deciding Advantageously Before Knowing the Advantageous Strategy," *Science* 275, no. 5304 (February 1997): 1293–95, doi:10.1126/science.275.5304.1293.

Page 78, *our physiology, or our bodily functions, can predict the correct answer*: Daryl J. Bem, "Feeling the Future: Experimental Evidence for Anomalous Retroactive Influences on Cognition and Affect," *Journal of Personality and Social Psychology* 100, no. 3 (March 2011): 407–25, doi:10.1037/a0021524.

Page 78, *"The theory of relativity occurred to me…"*: Shinichi Suzuki, *Nurtured by Love: A New Approach to Education*, trans. Waltraud Susuki (New York: Exposition Press, 1969), 90.

Page 78, *Placing subjects in a brain scanner*: Kerri Smith, "Neuroscience vs. Philosophy: Taking Aim at Free Will," *Nature* 477 (2011): 23–25: doi:10.1038/477023a.

Page 79, *A four- to seven-second advanced response*: Jeff Bollow, "How Fast Is Your Brain?" *The Phenomenal Experience* (blog), http://thephenomenalexperience.com/content/how-fast-is-your-brain, accessed September 20, 2017.

Page 79, *the heart has a precognitive sense of future events*: Chris Walton, "Does Your Heart Know Your Future? Check This Mind Boggling Research!" *Gamma Mindset* (blog), January 24, 2015, http://www.gammamindset.com/blog/does-your-heart-know-your-future-check-this-mind-boggling-research.

Page 80, *nearly all the brain's work is conducted*: Ezequiel Morsella et al., "Homing In on Consciousness in the Nervous System: An Action-Based Synthesis," *Behavioral and Brain Sciences* 39 (January 2016), doi:10.1017/S0140525X15000643.

Page 82, *The more comfortable I grew looking for nothing*: The mechanics of open focus, as well as many of my experiences employing this technique with patients, are explored at greater length in *Take Off Your Glasses and See: A Mind/Body Approach* (New York: Harmony, 1995).

Page 82, *"Everything you see has its roots..."*: Jalal ad-Din Rumi, in Will Johnson, *The Spiritual Practices of Rumi: Radical Techniques for Beholding the Divine* (Rochester, VT: Inner Traditions, 2007), chap. 2.

Page 83, *"The eye revolves upon an independent pivot..."*: Henry David Thoreau, cited in Arnold Gesell, Francis L. Ilg, and Glenna E. Bullis, *Vision: Its Development in Infant and Child* (New York: Paul B. Hoeber, 1949), 3.

Page 84, *"All great achievements of science must start from intuitive knowledge..."*: Albert Einstein, quoted in Leon Gunther, *The Physics of Music and Color* (New York: Springer Science and Business Media, 2011), 5.

Page 84, *50 percent of patents were the result*: Pagan Kennedy, "How to Cultivate the Art of Serendipity," *New York Times*, January 2, 2016, http://www.nytimes.com/2016/01/03/opinion/how-to-cultivate-the-art-of-serendipity.html?_r=0.

Page 84, *events can be logically connected by cause and effect*: "Synchronicity," Wikipedia, last modified September 15, 2017, https://en.m.wikipedia.org/wiki/Synchronicity.

Page 87, *"Your soul knows the geography of your destiny..."*: John O'Donohue, *Anam Cara: A Book of Celtic Wisdom* (New York: Harper Perennial, 1997), 57.

Chapter Eight: Awareness Is Curative

Page 90, *almost every radical remission cancer survivor*: Kelly Turner, "The Science behind Intuition," PsychologyToday.com, May 20, 2014, https://www.psychologytoday.com/blog/radical-remission/201405/the-science-behind-intuition.

Page 94, *Expanded consciousness, such as the intuition*: "Checkbox Medicine: Evidence versus Intuition," *Medical Economics*, June 25, 2012, http://medicaleconomics.modernmedicine.com/medical-economics/news/modernmedicine/modern-medicine-feature-articles/checkbox-medicine-evidence-ve.

Page 96, *"The eye through which I see God..."*: Meister Eckhart, cited in Gary Lachman, *The Secret Teachers of the Western World* (New York: Tarcher-Perigee, 2015), 222.

Page 97, *"I am not in the world…"*: Deepak Chopra, *Power, Freedom, and Grace: Living from the Source of Lasting Happiness* (San Rafael, CA: Amber-Allen Publishing, 2006).

Page 98, *"My notion would be that anything which possesses…"*: Plato, *The Dialogues of Plato*, trans B. Jowett, vol. 4, 3rd edition revised (London: Oxford University Press, 1892), http://oll.libertyfund.org/titles/plato -dialogues-vol-4-parmenides-theaetetus-sophist-statesman-philebus.

Page 98, *researchers found that 12 percent of cardiac arrest survivors*: Pim van Lommel et al., "Near-Death Experience in Survivors of Cardiac Arrest: A Prospective Study in the Netherlands," *Lancet* 358, no. 9298 (December 2001): 2039–45, doi:10.1016/S0140-6736(01)07100-8.

Page 98, *"Such evidence, we believe, fundamentally conflicts…"*: Edward Kelly and Emily Williams Kelly, *Irreducible Mind: Toward a Psychology for the 21st Century* (Lanham, MD: Rowman and Littlefield, 2009), 365.

Chapter Nine: What Takes Your Breath Away

Page 102, *the heart and the universe share the same shape*: Charles Muses and Arthur M. Young, eds., *Consciousness and Reality* (New York, Avon Book, 1983).

Page 102, *the heart, the breath, and the universe share the same*: Bob Whitehouse, "At the Heart of the Matter, What Do Heart, Breath, and Universe Have in Common?" *The Heart of Better Breathing* (blog), http://breatheheartfully .com/blog/?p=68.

Page 103, *"Spirit is not a mystical concept…"*: Alexander Lowen, *Joy: The Surrender to the Body and to Life* (New York: Penguin, 1995), 314.

Page 103, *"How do you tell if something's alive?…"*: Markus Zusak, *The Book Thief* (New York: Alfred A. Knopf, 2005), 38.

Page 104, *the average human has about seventy thousand thoughts per day*: "How Many Thoughts Do We Have per Minute?," Reference.com, https://www.reference.com/world-view/many-thoughts-per-minute -cb7fcf22ebbf8466#, accessed September 20, 2017.

Page 104, *"The intellect has little to do on the road to discovery…"*: Albert Einstein, quoted in *The Human Side of Scientists*, ed. Ralph E. Oesper (Cincinnati, OH: University of Cincinnati, 1975), 58.

Chapter Ten: The True Law of Attraction

Page 118, *when hydrogen gas is heated*: "Absorption/Emission Lines," Khan Academy, https://www.khanacademy.org/partner-content/nasa/measuring universe/spectroscopy/a/absorptionemission-lines, accessed September 20, 2017.

Page 119, *"One does not become fully human painlessly"*: Rollo May, foreword to *Existential-Phenomenological Alternatives for Psychology*, by Ronald S. Valle and Mark King (New York: Oxford University Press, 1978).

Page 122, *syntonics increases attention, learning, and memory*: "The Effect of Syntonic (Colored Light) Stimulation on Certain Visual and Cognitive Functions," *Journal of Optometric Vision Development* 17, no. 2 (June 1986): 4–15.

Page 125, *most scientists previously thought that people with normal vision*: Natalie Wolchover, "Your Color Red Really Could Be My Blue," *Live Science*, June 29, 2012, http://www.livescience.com/21275-color-red-blue-scientists.html.

Page 125, *Neitz and his colleagues injected the eyes of monkeys*: Katherine Mancuso et al., "Gene Therapy for Red–Green Colour Blindness in Adult Primates," *Nature* 461 (October 8, 2009): 784–87, doi:10.1038/nature08401.

Page 125, *"We are still on the threshold of fully understanding the complex relationship between light and life..."*: Fritz-Albert Popp, "Prof. Fritz-Albert Popp," Biontology Arizona, https://www.biontologyarizona.com/dr-fritz-albert-popp, accessed September 20, 2017.

Chapter Eleven: Full-Spectrum Life

Page 134, *"when a cell is in optimal health..."*: Fritz-Albert Popp, personal interview with author at the International Institute of Biophysics, Neuss, Germany, July 7, 1999.

Page 134, *the chakras are located at the site of the body's seven major endocrine glands*: Christopher Hills, personal conversations with author from 1983 to 1996.

Page 135, *"when a cell is out of balance, it responds to colors..."*: Fritz-Albert Popp, personal interview with author, July 7, 1999.

Page 135, *"mal-illumination"*: Jacob Liberman, *Light: Medicine of the Future* (Rochester, VT: Bear and Co., 1991), 51.

Chapter Twelve: Living in a World of Technology

Page 142, *children from eight to eighteen spend an average of seven hours*: Victoria J. Rideout, Ulla G. Foehr, and Donald F. Roberts, *Generation M²: Media in the Lives of 8- to 18-Year-Olds* (Menlo Park, CA: Henry J. Kaiser Family Foundation, 2010), 1, https://kaiserfamilyfoundation.files.wordpress.com /2013/01/8010.pdf?version=meter+at+2&module=meter-Links&pg type=Blogs&contentId=&mediaId=%25%25ADID%25%25&referrer=& priority=true&action=click&contentCollection=meter-links-click.

Page 142, *the diagnosis of attention deficit hyperactivity disorder (ADHD) has continued to rise*: Lesley Alderman, "Does Technology Cause ADHD?" *Everyday Health*, last modified August 31, 2010, http://www.everyday health.com/adhd-awareness/does-technology-cause-adhd.aspx.

Page 142, *exposure to screen media was associated with attention problems*: Edward L. Swing et al., "Television and Video Game Exposure and the Development of Attention Problems," *Pediatrics* 126, no. 2 (August 2010), http://pediatrics.aappublications.org/content/126/2/214.

Page 142, *all of us have become media frenzied*: Paul Pearsall, in Burl Burlingame, "New Book Takes Shine off Multitasking," *Honolulu Star-Bulletin*, July 15, 2002, http://www.paulpearsall.com/info/press/1.html.

Page 142, *everyday conversation between human beings is becoming increasingly rare*: Katherine Bindley, "When Children Text All Day, What Happens to Their Social Skills?" *Huffington Post*, last modified December 10, 2011, http://www.huffingtonpost.com/2011/12/09/children-texting-technology -social-skills_n_1137570.html.

Page 143, *some neuroscientists believe that use of the internet*: Fiona Macrae, "Facebook and Internet 'Can Re-wire Your Brain and Shorten Attention Span,'" *Daily Mail*, last modified September 15, 2010, http://www.daily mail.co.uk/sciencetech/article-1312119/Facebook-internet-wire-brain -shorten-attention-span.html#ixzz1ftJtJjF2.

Page 143, *In China, for instance, with its 1.2 billion cell phone users*: Jane E. Brody, "Screen Addiction Is Taking a Toll on Children," *Well* (blog), *New York Times*, July 5, 2015, http://well.blogs.nytimes.com/2015/07/06/screen -addiction-is-taking-a-toll-on-children/?_r=3.

Page 144, *internet gaming disorder is identified as a condition*: Stephanie Sarkis, "Internet Gaming Disorder in DSM-5," PsychologyToday.com, July 18, 2014, https://www.psychologytoday.com/blog/here-there-and-every where/201407/internet-gaming-disorder-in-dsm-5.

Page 146, *Any activity or environment that creates a mismatch*: S. Boyd Eaton, Melvin Konner, and Marjorie Shostak, "Stone Agers in the Fast Lane: Chronic Degenerative Diseases in Evolutionary Perspective," *American Journal of Medicine* 84, no. 4 (April 1988): 739–49.

Page 147, *up to 90 percent of young adults in China*: Alice Park, "Why Up to 90% of Asian Schoolchildren Are Nearsighted," *Time*, May 7, 2012, http://healthland.time.com/2012/05/07/why-up-to-90-of-asian-school children-are-nearsighted.

Page 147, *a 2009 National Eye Institute study that found an alarming 66 percent increase*: Susan Vitale, Robert D. Sperduto, and Frederick L. Ferris III, "Increased Prevalence of Myopia in the United States between 1971–1972 and 1999–2004," *JAMA Ophthalmology* 127, no. 12 (2009): 1632–39, doi:10.1001/archophthalmol.2009.303.

Page 147, *vision worsens in nearsighted children who spend less time outdoors*: Scott A. Read, Michael J. Collins, and Stephen J. Vincent, "Light Exposure and Eye Growth in Childhood," *Investigative Ophthalmology & Visual Science* 56, no. 11 (October 2015): 6779–87, doi:10.1167/iovs.14-15978.

Page 147, *Two-thirds of the US population wears glasses*: "Vision Facts and Statistics," MES Vision, https://www.mesvision.com/includes/pdf_Broker/MESVision%20Facts%20and%20Statistics.pdf, accessed September 20, 2017.

Page 147, *there are almost as many cell phone subscriptions (6.8 billion)*: Tim Fernholz, "More People around the World Have Cell Phones Than Ever Had Land-Lines," *Quartz*, February 25, 2014, https://qz.com/179897/more-people-around-the-world-have-cell-phones-than-ever-had-land-lines.

Page 148, *eye contact fully activates the parts of the brain*: Kate Murphy, "Psst. Look Over Here," *New York Times*, May 16, 2014, http://www.nytimes.com/2014/05/17/sunday-review/the-eyes-have-it.html?_r=0.

Page 149, *smartphones, laptops, televisions, LED lamps, and many other devices*: Fiona MacDonald, "Bright Light at Night Time Can Seriously Mess with Your Metabolism, Study Finds," *ScienceAlert*, May 20, 2016, http://www.sciencealert.com/checking-your-phone-at-night-could-be-messing-with-your-metabolism.

Page 149, *nighttime exposure to the same bright blue light*: Ivy N. Cheung et al., "Morning and Evening Blue-Enriched Light Exposure Alters Metabolic

Function in Normal Weight Adults," *PLOS ONE* 11, no. 5 (2016): e0155601, doi.org/10.1371/journal.pone.0155601.

Page 149, *83 percent of the world's population, and 99 percent of Europeans*: Fabio Falchi et al., "The New World Atlas of Artificial Night Sky Brightness," *Science Advances* 2, no. 6 (June 2016): e1600377, doi:10.1126 /sciadv.1600377.

Page 150, *"Twenty percent of the people in Europe…"*: Rebecca Morelle, "Light Pollution 'Affects 80% of Global Population,'" *BBC News*, June 10, 2016, http://www.bbc.com/news/science-environment-36492596.

Page 150, *several studies have proposed that exposing ourselves to artificial light*: Eva S. Schernhammer et al., "Rotating Night Shifts and Risk of Breast Cancer in Women Participating in the Nurses' Health Study," *JNCI: Journal of the National Cancer Institute* 93, no. 20 (October 2001): 1563–68, doi:10.1093/jnci/93.20.1563.

Page 150, *indicates a 30 to 50 percent increased risk of breast cancer*: Itai Kloog et al., "Nighttime Light Level Co-distributes with Breast Cancer Incidence Worldwide," *Cancer Causes & Control* 21, no. 12 (December 2010): 2059–68, doi:10.1007/s10552-010-9624-4.

Page 150, *young mice exposed to artificial light around the clock*: Eliane A. Lucas-sen et al., "Environmental 24-hr Cycles Are Essential for Health," *Current Biology* 26, no. 14 (July 2016): 1843–53, doi:10.1016/j.cub.2016.05.038.

Page 150, *too much light at night disrupts our natural sleep cycles*: Anahad O'Connor, "How Sleep Loss Adds to Weight Gain," *Well* (blog), *New York Times*, August 6, 2013, http://well.blogs.nytimes.com/2013/08/06 /how-sleep-loss-adds-to-weight-gain/?_r=1.

Page 150, *to heart disease*: "Insufficient Sleep Cycle — Especially for Shift Workers — May Increase Heart Disease Risk," American Heart Association, June 6, 2016, http://newsroom.heart.org/news/insufficient-sleep -cycle-especially-for-shift-workers-may-increase-heart-disease-risk.

Page 150, *cancer, and poor bone health*: Robert Preidt, "Sleep Apnea May Be Linked to Poor Bone Health," WebMD, April 15, 2014, http://www .webmd.com/sleep-disorders/sleep-apnea/news/20140415/sleep-apnea -may-be-linked-to-poor-bone-health.

Page 151, *brighter residential nighttime lighting is associated with less sleep*: "AMA Report Affirms Human Health Impacts from LEDs," Phys.org, June 22, 2016, https://phys.org/news/2016-06-ama-affirms-human-health -impacts.html.

Page 151, *Physicians at the 2016 annual meeting*: "AMA Adopts Guidance to Reduce Harm from High Intensity Street Lights," American Medical Association, June 14, 2016, https://www.ama-assn.org/ama-adopts-guidance-reduce-harm-high-intensity-street-lights.

Chapter Thirteen: Looking Less, Seeing More

Page 156, *the "socially compulsive, near-centered visual tasks"*: Martin H. Birnbaum, *Optometric Management of Nearpoint Vision Disorders* (Santa Ana, CA: Butterworth-Heinemann, 2008).

Page 156, *patients who looked at one spot with their eyes but elsewhere*: Arnold Gesell, Francis L. Ilg, and Glenna E. Bullis, *Vision: Its Development in Infant and Child* (New York: Paul B. Hoeber, 1949), 183.

Page 156, *vision was designed to be effortless*: Jacob Liberman, "Prescribing for Performance and Prevention," *Journal of the American Optometric Association* 47, no. 8 (August 1976): 1058–64.

Page 157, *using this device ten minutes a day, over a three-week period*: Hannu Laukkanen and Jeff Rabin, "A Prospective Study of the EYEPORT Vision Training System," *Optometry* 77, no. 10 (October 2006): 508–14.

Page 157, *using this device on the batting performance*: Teresa Bowen and Lisa Horth, "Use of the EYEPORT™ Vision Training System to Enhance the Visual Performance of Little League Baseball Players," *Journal of Behavioral Optometry* 16, no. 6 (2005): 143–48.

Page 157, *A third study was conducted in 2005 with the Maui County Police Department*: Jacob Liberman and Lisa Horth, "Use of the EYEPORT Vision Training System to Enhance the Visual Performance of Police Recruits: A Pilot Study," *Journal of Behavioral Optometry* 17, no. 4 (2006): 87–92.

Page 158, *a pilot study conducted in 2007 at Northeastern State University*: Hanni Hagen, Kari Moore, Gary Wickham, and W. C. Maples, "Effect of the EYEPORT® System on Visual Function in ADHD Children: A Pilot Study," *Journal of Behavioral Optometry* 19, no. 2 (2008): 37–41.

Chapter Fourteen: What's Catching Your Eye?

Page 169, *"The baby looks at things all day without blinking…"*: Zhuangzi, quoted in Bruce Lee and John Little, *Bruce Lee: Artist of Life* (North Clarenden, VT: Tuttle, 2001), 6.

Page 170, *Once these viewpoints are processed in the visual cortex*: Jenny Read,

"Early Computational Processing in Binocular Vision and Depth Perception," *Progress in Biophysics and Molecular Biology* 87, no. 1 (January 2005): 77–108, doi:10.1016/j.pbiomolbio.2004.06.005.

Page 170, *"the crown jewel of organic evolution"*: Arnold Gesell, Francis L. Ilg, and Glenna E. Bullis, *Vision: Its Development in Infant and Child* (New York: Paul B. Hoeber, 1949), 3.

Page 171, *"The Great Way is not difficult..."*: Seng-Ts'an, *Hsin-Hsin Ming: Verses on the Faith-Mind*, trans. Richard B. Clarke (Buffalo, NY: White Pine Press, 2001).

Page 172, *when monkeys are placed in a visually confined environment*: Francis A. Young, "The Development of Myopia," *Contacto* 15, no. 1 (1971): 36–42.

Page 172, *Navy submarine personnel, working in a confined visual environment*: Ira Schwartz and N. Elaine Sandberg, "The Effect of Time in Submarine Service on Vision," *Naval Submarine Medical Research Laboratory Report*, no. 253 (Falls Church, VA: Bureau of Medicine and Surgery, Navy Department, 1954).

Page 172, *Yet in another study conducted on indigenous cultures*: Francis A. Young et al., "The Transmission of Refractive Errors within Eskimo Families," *American Journal of Optometry and Archives of the American Academy of Optometry* 46, no. 9 (1969): 676–85.

Page 172, *"If the eye should become excessively specialized..."*: Gesell, Ilg, and Bullis, *Vision*, 32.

Epilogue

Page 179, *"The scientific picture of the real world around me..."*: Erwin Schrödinger, *Nature and the Greeks* (Cambridge, UK: Cambridge University Press, 1954), 95.

RESOURCES

College of Optometrists in Vision Development: www.covd.org

College of Syntonic Optometry: www.collegeofsyntonicoptometry.com

International Light Association: www.international-light-association.org

The Optometric Extension Program Foundation: www.oepf.org

INDEX

ABOUT THE AUTHORS

*D*r. Jacob Israel Liberman is a pioneer in the fields of light, vision, and consciousness and the author of *Light: Medicine of the Future* and *Take Off Your Glasses and See*. He earned a doctorate in optometry from Southern College of Optometry and a PhD in vision science from the College of Syntonic Optometry, and was awarded an honorary doctorate of science from the Open International University for Complementary Medicines. He is a past president of the College of Syntonic Optometry and the International Society for the Study of Subtle Energies and Energy Medicine and a fellow emeritus of the American Academy of Optometry, College of Syntonic Optometry, College of Optometrists in Vision Development, and International Academy of Color Sciences. He received the H. R. Spitler Award for his contributions to the field of phototherapy and has invented numerous light therapy devices, including the first FDA-cleared medical device to significantly improve overall visual performance. A respected public speaker, he shares his scientific and spiritual discoveries with audiences worldwide. He lives in Maui, Hawaii.

Gina Liberman is a poet, counselor, and artist living in Charleston, South Carolina.

Erik Liberman in an award-winning actor, writer, and director living in New York City.